Go For It!

25 Faith-Building Adventures for Groups

by Walt Marcum

ABINGDON PRESS
NASHVILLE

About the Author

Walt Marcum is an ordained pastor in The United Methodist Church, currently serving at Highland Park United Methodist Church, in Dallas, Texas. He has been working with youth since 1968, as a volunteer, as a pastor, and—since 1986—as a minister to youth. Walt lives with his wife, Barbara, who is also an ordained minister, and with his daughter, Melissa, who is in the youth program. Walt enjoys writing, teaching, and working with youth and with adults who work with youth. Walt's ambition is to be the world's oldest practicing youth minister. Currently, he is on track to meet that goal.

Dedication

To the youth, parents, and volunteers at Highland Park United Methodist Church whose openness to new ideas and forms of ministry have led to the activities in this book becoming an important part of our ministry together.

Acknowledgments

A special thanks to Billy and Laura Echols-Richter, who introduced me to the world of ropes-challenge initiatives. Their creativity serves as a constant source of inspiration to many of us in youth ministry.

Thanks also to the following youth from Highland Park Church (they had a good time doing the Adventures so that we could take their photos!):

Rebecca Ensley, Lane Evans, Jessica Findley, John Flowers, Beth Hahn, Krissi Holman, Gray Hughes, Carrie Johnson, Hannah Kohler, Stacie Lea, Samantha Linsley, Sean Rudin, Katie Wilson, Sheba Wilson, Zimo Zheng

Contents

Welcome to Adventure Learning!

A Word From Walt

The activities in **GO FOR IT! 25 FAITH-BUILDING ADVENTURES FOR GROUPS** reflect one of the cutting edges of contemporary youth ministry. Many of us have had the joy of going to ropes challenge courses and participating in their challenge initiatives. Those of us who have done this know the teaching value of these activities.

If adventure learning is new to you, the sessions that follow may seem unusual and different. They don't look like what we have done in traditional Christian education. But to capture the attention of youth today and stimulate their growth in faith, you may be ready for something different.

Most of the activities you will find in this book are not new. Many of them have been around for years. (See "Where to Go for More," page 94.) What is new for many of us is not the activities themselves but the ways to use them in a comprehensive Christian education program with youth. Adventure learning has ceased to be something that we have to go away to experience at a camp or retreat center. Adventure learning has come into the church classroom.

> **Adventure learning has come into the church classroom.**

The Origin of Adventure Learning

I first encountered adventure learning about fifteen years ago when I took a youth council to a ropes challenge course. What I experienced at that retreat was a shift in how I thought about teaching youth. As I watched the trained facilitators work with our youth on the elements and observed how they debriefed each experience, I marveled. The Christian education value of both the activities and the debriefing discussions was clear.

For years we made an annual trek to the ropes course. This experience was a highlight of our youth ministry program.

Some of the finest leadership development for youth I have ever encountered has been in the ropes-course setting with its challenge initiatives. I also began to hear from parents and volunteers that many corporations and businesses were using ropes courses to train their executive leadership and sales teams.

We began to do some of the low elements in our own church. We adapted many of the exercises to new situations; and finally, we began to create our own challenge initiatives, keeping in mind the local church setting.

Over a period of several years many of these activities began to move into our curriculum. First we used them at retreats, then we used them at our evening fellowship meetings, and most recently we began to use them in summer Sunday school.

Why Summer Sunday School?

The decision to use these activities in Sunday school began in 1995 in our confirmation class. We promoted our fifth graders into the sixth-grade confirmation class at the first of June, but we didn't start the traditional curriculum until mid-August. We were looking for a curriculum that would help us mold the new confirmation class members into a community. What we needed were activities that would teach communication, cooperation, and teamwork.

Our other need was for each session to stand alone. The youth of our church are in and out throughout the summer. Any curriculum that assumed continuity would not work.

The lower elements used at ropes challenge courses were ideal. They were active and fun; each one stood alone, and they taught basic Christian principles. The problem was that they were just activities.

As the activities are commonly used, they do not meet our expectations for Sunday school. The Sunday morning opportunity for Christian education is too short for just activity—no matter how fun! In Sunday school we want activities that create dialogue with the faith and with the Bible.

In 1995 I worked about fifteen of these activities into a class format (see pages 12–13) and we used them for our summer curriculum for our sixth-graders. The results were phenomenal:

☼ Our attendance shot up.

☼ Class members told their parents how much fun Sunday school was.

☼ They began bringing their friends.

☼ Stories surfaced of youth who did not want to go on vacations or on trips because they would miss Sunday school.

☼ Parents and other adults who lead these activities sang the format's praises, both in terms of how much their youth were enjoying the class sessions and in terms of their teaching content.

☼ And, when we talked with the class members, they could clearly connect what we were doing with the basic principles of our faith.

The next summer we expanded the number of activities and extended this format two more grades. The material in this book now represents the summer Sunday school curriculum at Highland Park United Methodist Church for grades six, seven, and eight.

But Is This Christian Education?

The activities you will find in this curriculum are fun. Youth love them. But is this Christian education? To be honest, the answer is both no and yes.

The answer is no in the sense that the activities—by themselves—do not produce the results we want in Christian education. By themselves they are probably more recreation than anything else. It's worth remembering that simply doing an activity—by itself—does not guarantee learning. Just because we teach (whatever the form—lecture, learning centers, or challenge initiatives) does not mean that anyone is learning anything.

The answer is yes, though, because of the crucial element of reflection. An experience can be powerful, but it becomes educational when opportunities to debrief and to make new links are intentional. Experience + integration = learning. This is why what surrounds the activity is so important. Each adventure in Go For It! contains not only a Debrief for the activity but also a Faith Link. This Faith Link uses Scripture and questions to link the experience and the learning that has taken place to our faith in Jesus Christ.

What's Important

Don't worry about "finishing" a particular activity. With adventure learning it is a mistake to skip the Debrief and Faith Link elements so that the youth will have time to finish an exercise. Missing the debriefing and linking opportunities results in the class members having a lot of fun, but not growing spiritually. When this happens, we are in recreational ministry—not Christian education. We need to allow enough time to do these exercises. But we also need to not be afraid to stop an exercise in order to learn from it. Always reserve time for the Debrief and the Faith Link segments.

Let your questions arise out of the experience itself. One of the most powerful lessons I have learned as an educator happened as I watched trained ropes leaders debrief the group. No one can anticipate what will or not happen when a group does one of these exercises. Each time is unique. Even if the same group repeats the exercise, it will be different.

The questions found in this curriculum are only suggestions. They are there to get you started. The real debriefing begins when you watch your group do the exercise, observe what does or does not happen, and then—through your questions—have the group reflect on the meaning of the activity and on how that meaning is connected to our faith as Christians.

I look back on the years of using these activities with youth, and I see clearly their contribution to the spiritual growth of young people. I share this resource with you in the prayerful hope that you too will see the results you desire in the name of Jesus Christ.

Go for it!

Walt Marcum
Dallas, Texas
1998

Wanted: Adventuresome Adults

The activities in this book are adult-intensive in two ways:

1. *Many of the activities will be done in small groups of about eight. You will need a minimum of one adult with each small group. Other adults can participate in the activity and join in the debriefing.*

2. *Some of the activities have physical safety issues. All of them have emotional safety issues. One of the roles the adults play is that of a guarantor of safety. Not having enough adults to adequately supervise the activity can be unsafe —both emotionally and physically. It is worth the time and effort to make sure that you have enough adults present and that they know what the leaders are doing.*

Adults—Get Involved!

No spectators! If at all possible, do the activity with the youth. If you physically cannot do a particular activity, that is fine. Just make sure that you are involved in support. We adults should not be apart from the group or uninvolved. That gives the class members an excuse not to be involved. We lead by example, by modeling.

We do what we ask them to do.

We do what we ask them to do.

Training Your Volunteers

The best way to train your adults is to have them do the activity themselves as a group. Take the adults through the exercise before they lead others in it. Debrief with the adults just as you want them to do with the youth. Then talk together about leading the youth through the experience.

This method of training will

- help your leaders know how to set up the activity and run it;
- give you opportunity to clarify the directions in response to their questions or concerns;
- model the discussion techniques you want them to use with the youth;
- give your leaders confidence.

In addition, having done the activity, the adult team can then strategize how to get the most from the activity. They may also have ideas as to how to improve the setup in the particular location.

Finally, safety should always be your first concern. It is unsafe to have adults leading youth in an activity they have not done themselves.

Safety 1st

Emotional safety is a major concern in all of the exercises. For many people (both youth and adults) these activities are new and different. By design, they push participants beyond their normal comfort zone. They involve an element of risk. This pushing of the comfort zone is intentional, but it must be balanced with safety.

To ensure emotional safety, practice "challenge by choice." Do not force anyone to do an exercise. For persons who are unsure, have them watch others do the exercise. Then give them another opportunity. They may then be willing. Encourage everyone to try the activity, but clearly communicate that the ultimate decision is up to the particular person.

If someone decides that the activity is too scary, he or she can still participate—but in a different way. Spotting to ensure the safety of others and encouraging others do not require doing anything scary. Do not allow reluctant persons to remove themselves from the group completely. They are still needed—by the others.

Physical safety is mostly a matter of common sense. A few of these activities involve physical risk. Any activity in which a person leaves the ground has an element of risk. In particular, Escape From Auschwitz, Eye of the Needle, Spider Web, and the Trust Exercises all involve lifting people off the ground. Other exercises, such as Islands, River Crossing, and The Welcome, involve the group being at least a few inches off the ground.

When you set up the activity and train your adults, think safety. Is the equipment safe? Will platforms and ropes hold enough weight? If you have gym mats, or other mats, you may want to place them in any location where there is even a possibility that a person may fall.

Train your adults to be spotters. The role of a spotter is to ensure that if a person were to fall or be dropped, he or she would not hit the floor and be injured. Have extra adults ready to offer a steadying hand when needed. Youth can also spot.

Teaching for Thinking

An old story has been traveling around in Christian education circles for some time. In this story a Sunday school teacher calls on Johnny. The trouble is that Johnny has not been paying attention. He has been having a rather delightful conversation with his friend next to him (which is probably why the teacher called on him in the first place). Johnny knows that the teacher expects him to answer, but he has no idea what the teacher asked.

But Johnny is savvy. He is a seasoned veteran of Sunday school. So he responds, "I don't know what the question is, but I know the answer you want is 'Jesus.' "

This story captures a sad truth: In many Christian education settings we don't encourage or challenge youth to think. We expect certain "correct" answers.

Adventure education requires its participants to think. The challenge requires them to solve a problem. The debriefing questions push them to make connections; but no one can know the answers in advance because the exercise is different every time. Even doing the same exercise two times in a row with the same group will produce different results. The teaching content remains the same, but what participants learn will vary widely.

4 Ways to Encourage Thinking

1. Create an environment of openness. From the very beginning, let the participants know that you will be asking them to think for themselves and problem-solve. Youth will find this approach exciting and energizing.

2. Ask open-ended and feeling questions. An open-ended question is one that is difficult to respond to with a yes, no, or other brief answer. "How old are you?" "Fifteen." "Did you like the activity?" "Yes." Questions such as these produce closed answers.

In contrast, open-ended questions invite persons to reflect on their experience and to talk about their feelings and insights. "What was that like for you?" "What did you notice?" These are open-ended questions.

Questions such as, "What was that like for you?" invite youth to talk about their feelings. "How did that make you feel?" "What did you find scary?" are even more direct. The questions given in the sessions are only suggestions. The best questions are the ones you come up with as you watch your group do the activity.

3. Keep the discussions open ended. Not only can a question be open ended, but a discussion can be too. An open-ended discussion is one in which there is no one right answer. We are not looking for "Jesus" as the only correct answer! We are asking participants to process their own experiences, think critically, and listen and respond to the experience and thinking of others. This kind of discussion may be harder to lead, but it is also more rewarding.

The questions in the sessions are good starting points. The answers to these will raise other questions. Many different learnings are possible from each activity. A teachable moment will likely arise from the activity, but we can never be sure what the moment will be or what the teaching will be. Often, several opportunities will arise from one activity. Adventure learning is rich in its ability to create these moments.

4. Encourage and accept all answers. Some will be off the wall, but the group and the process will moderate these and filter them. Some exercises and discussions will generate more questions than answers. This result is not undesirable. Life is not tied up with a neat little bow. Reality is not a TV drama. We don't solve the problems of the world (or in the activity) in 30 minutes.

We want our youth to encounter problems and issues, struggle with them, and learn. On a good day, answers come. Most days, simply having the group gain insight into the nature of what we are teaching is a notable accomplishment.

Raising more questions than answers forces the participants to think. Taking an issue seriously and struggling with it are first steps toward finding a solution. Adventure learning seeks not so much to give answers as to teach problem-solving skills.

Work to include everyone in the discussion—even the quiet and shy members.

Experience by itself does not necessarily teach. But when we reflect on our experience, draw meaning from it, and begin to apply this insight in our lives, then learning has taken place.

Adventure learning is interactive. This kind of education assumes that each of the participants has something to offer and that the interaction among them intensifies the learning. Insight does not come from the leader, but from the participants. During that all-important Debrief and Faith Link, the leader's role is to facilitate discussion—not to give answers.

> **The key to learning from these activities is reflecting on the experience.**

3 Sure-fire Techniques

Once a discussion is going, it is relatively easy to maintain. The difficult part of leading a discussion is getting started. Having a few good discussion techniques up your sleeve is always a good idea. Here are a few that work well in the adventure-learning setting:

1. Power Ball: Have the group sit in a circle and have a small object ready (a ball; a wad of paper; a small, light object used in the exercise). Tell the group that you are going to have a Power Ball discussion.

Say: "Whoever has the ball (wad, whatever) has the power—the power to talk. Only the person who has the ball can talk. Everyone else must listen. When the ball comes to you, you must talk. You cannot pass. How long or how briefly you talk is up to you. But you must answer the question or speak to the issue.

"You also have the power to decide who will speak next. When you are ready, toss the ball to someone else in the circle. People can indicate they want to speak by raising their hand, but you have the power. You decide who speaks next."

Toss the ball to a group member and ask the first question. He or she can then throw the ball to someone else for that person to respond. When you are ready, ask a new question (usually as the ball is tossed to another person).

2. Continuum: Have the group express their answers on a continuum. Have one side of an area represent one side of an issue. The other side of an area represents the other side of an issue. Participants can place themselves anywhere on the continuum. Make sure that your question can be answered on a continuum. One example would be:

"How scared were you while we were doing this exercise? This side represents terrified. This side represents not scared at all. You can be anywhere on the continuum."

Be sure to ask several people why they placed themselves where they did. Try to get perspectives from the two extremes. Have the participants at one end explain their position to people at the other end.

3. Insider/Outsider: If the exercise results in two different groups or two different kinds of experience, you may want to use this exercise. This is also known as a "fishbowl' exercise. In Insider/Outsider you will want one group (or part of a group) to form an inside circle so that they can talk, while the rest of the group sits in a second circle outside the first group and listens.

This technique is particularly helpful if you feel that one group is not listening to the other group or if you feel that one group is feeling left out. Insider/Outsider possibilities include: girls and guys, older and younger, new members of the group and veterans, those who were leaders in the exercise and those who were followers, those who dominated and those who were dominated, those who were talkative and those who were quiet, or simply those who volunteer for the circles.

Have Yarn, Will Travel:
Basic Equipment and Cheap Substitutes

Each Adventure has its own list of supplies or equipment. However, many of the items are common to more than one activity. As you gather materials for each of your group's initial Adventures, you are adding to your storehouse for the next ones.

You do not have to spend a lot of money to get appropriate supplies. Be creative, if need be. Here are some simple substitutes; you also will see others.

> **A trip to a toy store can give you lots of ideas for supplies.**

- Rope, yarn, and bungee cords are often interchangeable.
- Bungee cords (elastic cords with hooks on both ends) are a good investment and can make setting up the various Adventures much easier, but they are not essential.
- Balls can be bean bags or paper wads.
- Blindfolds can be bandannas (newly purchased) or strips of clean, discarded cloth.
- Blocks can be concrete or wooden; bricks make good substitutes.
- Obstacles can be whatever appropriate-size items are on hand; for example, tables, chairs, balls, books. However, consider purchasing some of the colorful floating pool toys ("noodles") that fit together in a variety of configurations.

Summer Sunday School: A Sample Class Format

Purposes

To build community in a fun environment
To bond class members to one another as well as to our teaching team
To raise important faith issues
To connect our experiences with our faith

Welcome

Our first objective is to make everyone feel welcome. Because ours is a large class, we have the participants sign in and we give them a nametag. We take their picture if they are new and add it to the others of our class members.

Singing

We sing three or four songs with guitar accompaniment. Some of our youth play and help lead the singing.

Prayer Time

We allow time for persons to express prayer concerns and joys. We follow each one with, "This is our prayer, O Lord." Then we end with the Lord's Prayer. This is a community-building activity as well as a teaching tool for helping the class members grow in their comfort level with prayer, especially praying aloud.

Challenge Activity

We use this activity to help class members experience being a part of a community of faith. All of the initiatives require working together as a group. After being given the initiative, the class members do not automatically jump in and make an attempt. They are to sit down and take a few minutes to problem-solve and come up with a plan for attacking the problem. Once they are in agreement about what they are to do, they can proceed. Participants learn to cooperate, to contribute, to problem-solve, to trust one another, and to respect the uniqueness of the other members. Following the activity, we use the debriefing questions to begin reflecting upon the experience.

Faith Link

We are not just a group, but a Christian community of faith. We read the chosen Scripture and give the participants the opportunity to connect the Word with their experience in the activity. The questions help them reflect on the activity in light of their faith and their faith in light of the activity.

The key Christian teaching for the summer is Paul's analogy about the body (1 Corinthians 12:12-27), which explores what it means to be a community of faith. Our entire summer session attempts to embody what Paul discusses in this passage. In addition, each week we refer to other specific Scriptures to link to more specific faith topics.

1 Corinthians 12:12-27

For just as the body is one and has many members, and all the members of the body, though many, are one body, so it is with Christ. For in the one Spirit we were all baptized into one body—Jews or Greeks, slaves or free—and we were all made to drink of one Spirit. Indeed, the body does not consist of one member but of many. If the foot would say, "Because I am not a hand, I do not belong to the body," that would not make it any less a part of the body. And if the ear would say, "Because I am not an eye, I do not belong to the body," that would not make it any less a part of the body. If the whole body were an eye, where would the hearing be? If the whole body were hearing, where would the sense of smell be? But as it is, God arranged the members in the body, each one of them, as he chose. If all were a single member, where would the body be? As it is, there are many members, yet one body. The eye cannot say to the hand, "I have no need of you," nor again the head to the feet, "I have no need of you." On the contrary, the members of the body that seem to be weaker are indispensable, and those members of the body that we think less honorable we clothe with greater honor, and our less respectable members are treated with respect; whereas our more respectable members do not need this. But God has so arranged the body, giving the greater honor to the inferior member, that there may be no dissension within the body, but the members may have the same care for one another. If one member suffers, all suffer together with it; if one member is honored, all rejoice together with it. Now you are the body of Christ and individually members of it.

Closing

Each week we end by standing in a circle, holding hands, making any closing announcements, and then saying together the traditional benediction (from Numbers 6:24-26):

The LORD bless you and keep you;
the LORD make his face to shine upon you, and be gracious to you;
the LORD lift up his countenance upon you, and give you peace.
[Amen.]

This format is what Highland Park United Methodist Church (Dallas, Texas) uses as its Sunday school program for the summer. They use the challenge activities and faith links in Go For It. You may wish to add your own opening and a closing ritual when you use adventure learning with your group.

Abraham's Journey

Focus: *Faith, trust, discernment*

Core Teaching: *Christian discipleship is a journey of faith. It involves trust. It also involves discernment—trying to figure out what God would have us do, what God is calling us to. That is not always clear. We need to interpret what we hear God saying; a community of faith can help. Understanding these things will give us a clearer insight into the story of Abraham and into our own walk with God.*

Scripture: *Genesis 12:1-9 (Abram trusts God's leading.)*

Now the LORD said to Abram, "Go from your country and your kindred and your father's house to the land that I will show you. I will make of you a great nation, and I will bless you, and make your name great, so that you will be a blessing. I bless those who bless you, and the one who curses you I will curse; and in you all the families of the earth shall be blessed."

So Abram went, as the LORD had told him; and Lot went with him. Abram was seventy-five years old when he departed from Haran. Abram took his wife Sarai and his brother's son Lot, and all the possessions that they had gathered, and the persons whom they had acquired in Haran; and they set forth to go to the land of Canaan. When they had come to the land of Canaan, Abram passed through the land to the place at Shechem, to the oak of Moreh. At that time the Canaanites were in the will land. Then the LORD appeared to Abram, and said, "To your offspring I will give this land." So he built there an altar to the LORD, who had appeared to him. From there he moved on to the hill country on the east of Bethel, and pitched his tent, with Bethel on the west and Ai on the east; and there he built an altar to the LORD and invoked the name of the LORD. And Abram journeyed on by stages toward the Negeb.

1 Samuel 3:1-10 (Samuel hears God's call.)

Now the boy Samuel was ministering to the LORD under Eli. The word of the LORD was rare in those days; visions were not widespread. At that time Eli, whose eyesight had begun to grow dim so that he could not see, was lying down in his room; the lamp of God had not yet gone out, and Samuel was lying down in the temple of the LORD, where the ark of God was. Then the LORD called, "Samuel! Samuel!" and he said, "Here I am!" and ran to Eli, and said, "Here I am, for you called me." But he said, "I did not call; lie down again." So he went and lay down. The LORD called again, "Samuel!" Samuel got up and went to Eli, and said, "Here I am, for you called me." But he said, "I did not call, my son; lie down again." Now Samuel did not yet know the LORD, and the word of the LORD had not yet been revealed to him. The LORD called Samuel again, a third time. And he got up and went to Eli, and said, "Here I am, for you called me." Then Eli perceived that the LORD was calling the boy. Therefore Eli said to Samuel, "Go, lie down; and if he calls you, you shall say, 'Speak, LORD, for your servant is listening.'" So Samuel went and lay down in his place. Now the LORD came and stood there, calling as before, "Samuel! Samuel!" And Samuel said, "Speak, for your servant is listening."

Group Size:

Small groups of no more than 8, plus one adult guide; additional adults to monitor for safety

Space: Indoors or outdoors; a route

Supplies or Equipment: Blindfolds; obstacles

Preparation

☐ Choose or create the route that you want your "Abrahams" to wander through.
☐ Outdoors, be sure the path has plenty of obstacles that the group will need to go over, under, though, or around.
☐ Indoors, you will need fewer obstacles since the building itself will complicate the path.
☐ Use halls and various rooms to make the route at least 100 yards. The route should not be easy.
☐ Make sure your leaders understand the exercise.
☐ Prepare them for their role as guides. In communicating with their "family," they may not touch anyone, nor can they use words. Whistles, clucking, clapping, and so forth are acceptable means of communication.

The Challenge

The challenge is for each group to listen for and figure out (discern) what they are being called to do, and then to follow through.

The Process

Take everyone to a location near where you will be doing Abraham's Journey. Blindfold the participants.

Read aloud Genesis 12:1-3, then say:

"Welcome to Abraham's journey. Today we will be wandering through the wilderness to a place we cannot see. The journey will not be easy. It will have many obstacles. Your group will be journeying together, just as Abraham's family did. Just as Abraham had God's guiding, you will have someone to guide you. That voice will safely lead you to your goal.

"The problem is that God's voice is not always clear or easy to understand. You will have to listen closely and discern God's voice from the other sounds around you. You will also have to figure out what the voice is saying and what it means, and then follow it."

Assign the guides. Give the groups three minutes to get organized, establish communication, and begin the journey.

Allow 25–30 minutes for the groups to complete the task.

Debrief

Debrief the groups either together or individually. One consideration is that each group will probably finish at a different time. So you may want the guides to debrief their own group. Have the participants remove their blindfolds and sit in a circle. Then ask:

- What was the experience like for you?
- What was difficult about this experience?
- What were the keys to success?
- How difficult was it to know where the instructions were coming from?
- How difficult was it for you to understand the instructions you were receiving?
- How were you able to discern the meaning of what you were hearing?

Faith Link

Have a volunteer read aloud Genesis 12:1-9, then ask:

- What insight does the exercise we just did give you into the Abraham story?
- What did God really ask Abraham to do?
- How hard do you think this was for Abraham?
- How hard would it be for you?
- In real life, how do God's voice and guidance come to us?
- How do we discern God's voice from all of the other voices around us?
- How do we understand what God is saying to us?
- From this experience what insight do you have about your own walk with God?

Have a volunteer read aloud 1 Samuel 3:1-10, then ask:

- How did Samuel finally figure out that it was God who was speaking to him?
- Who or what plays that role in our own lives?

Whistle, cluck, or clap to communicate.

SNAP! SNAP!

The Abyss

Supplies or Equipment:
Two chairs, yarn or string, masking tape

Focus: *Working through adversity*

Core Teaching: *Often in life we seek to avoid adversity. However, the things that make us struggle and work harder—even our sufferings—can have a positive side. Working through our difficulties shapes us, strengthens us, and forms our character.*

Scripture: *Isaiah 48:10 (I have refined you.)*

See, I have refined you, but not like silver; I have tested you in the furnace of adversity.

Romans 5:3-5 (Suffering leads to hope.)

And not only that, but we also boast in our sufferings, knowing that suffering produces endurance, and endurance produces character, and character produces hope, and hope does not disappoint us, because God's love has been poured into our hearts through the Holy Spirit that has been given to us.

2 Corinthians 4:8-16a (We are not forsaken.)

We are afflicted in every way, but not crushed; perplexed, but not driven to despair; persecuted, but not forsaken; struck down, but not destroyed; always carrying in the body the death of Jesus, so that the life of Jesus may also be made visible in our bodies. For while we live, we are always being given up to death for Jesus' sake, so that the life of Jesus may be made visible in our mortal flesh. So death is at work in us, but life in you. But just as we have the same spirit of faith that is in accordance with scripture—"I believed, and so I spoke"—we also believe, and so we speak, because we know that the one who raised the Lord Jesus will raise us also with Jesus, and will bring us with you into his presence. Yes, everything is for your sake, so that grace, as it extends to more and more people, may increase thanksgiving, to the glory of God. So we do not lose heart.

Group Size: small groups of 8–10 with at least one adult leader

Space: Indoors

Preparation

☐ Place two chairs about six feet apart.
☐ Tie a string between the chairs about 24 inches high. To increase the difficulty, go as low as 18 inches.
☐ Tape two pieces of masking tape on the floor parallel to the string—each about three feet away from the string.
☐ Add a third piece of tape exactly below the string.

You will have created a zone about six feet square with the string in the center about 18 to 24 inches above the floor. The floor between the chairs and the two pieces of tape is "The Abyss"—a bottomless pit.

The Challenge

Tell the group they are in an Indiana Jones-type situation ("Indiana Jones and the Abyss"). They are in a cave trying to escape. A huge boulder is rolling toward them in the distance. There is only one way out. But it is blocked by the Abyss. The goal is for the entire group to make it safely across the Abyss before the boulder of death strikes (*rumble, rumble, rumble . . .*).

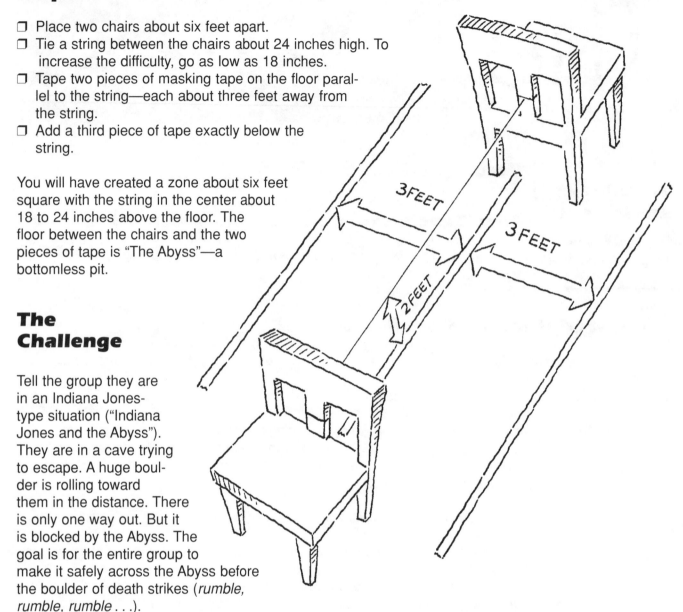

3 FEET

3 FEET

2 FEET

The Process

Give the group the following information to help them decide what to do:

The Abyss is six feet wide and has an opening only 18 to 24 inches tall, which rules out jumping. If persons put weight on the floor between the pieces of tape, they will "fall to their death." There is one "razor-sharp rock" in the center (the third piece of tape). The participants may brace with the bottoms of their shoes on that rock, but they may not use their hands. The rock will cut off their hands. Only the bottoms of their shoes can stand up to that sharp rock.

Debrief

Have the group sit in a circle around the Abyss, then ask:

- What was this exercise like for you?
- What was difficult about this experience?
- What did you try that did not work?
- What did you try that did work?
- What were the keys to success?
- How was the first person able to cross the Abyss?
- How did you get the last person across the Abyss?

Faith Link

Have persons read aloud the Scripture passages, then ask:

- What is the point of the Scriptures we just read?
- What do the Scriptures say about the role of adversity and suffering in our lives?
- What does the exercise we just completed have to do with what the Scriptures are saying?
- What do you think about this connection?
- What experiences have you had with suffering?
- How has suffering or adversity strengthened you or made you grow?
- How does your suffering make you more sensitive to the suffering of others?

Bear One Another's Burdens

Focus: *Giving and receiving support*

Core Teaching: *As the people of God, we are called to "bear one another's burdens," to help one another. We give and receive support at many levels: physically, emotionally, morally, financially. Supporting one another is an important part of what it means to be "the body of Christ."*

Supplies or Equipment:

8–10 one and one-half-inch wooden dowels, each 42 inches long. Your local lumber yard should have these available.

Scripture: *Ephesians 4:1-7 (One body, one Spirit)*

I therefore, the prisoner in the Lord, beg you to lead a life worthy of the calling to which you have been called, with all humility and gentleness, with patience, bearing with one another in love, making every effort to maintain the unity of the Spirit in the bond of peace. There is one body and one Spirit, just as you were called to the one hope of your calling, one Lord, one faith, one baptism, one God and Father of all, who is above all and through all and in all. But each of us was given grace according to the measure of Christ's gift.

Galatians 6:2 (Bear one another's burdens.)

Bear one another's burdens, and in this way you will fulfill the law of Christ.

Group Size: *For Lap Sit: from 10 to 100; for the other two challenges: groups of 8–12*

Space: *Indoors or outdoors*

Preparation

❏ Today's session is a series of three challenges. Do one challenge, debrief it, and then do the next one.
❏ Do the Faith Link at the conclusion of all three challenges.

1st Challenge: Lap Sit

Have the group form a tight circle by linking arms. Then have them all turn right (or left—your choice, so long as they all turn the same way). Have them place their hands around the waist of the person in front of them. On the count of three, they are to sit on the lap behind them while the person in front of them sits in their lap.

You may want to do a trial run by having everyone go down on a 3-2-1 count so that they just touch the lap behind them and then stand up again. In this way they can make any adjustments they need. The key is for the circle to be very tight and round. Any gaps or kinks in the circle will result in part (or all) of the circle collapsing. It may take several attempts before being successful.

Debrief

Have the group sit in a circle, then ask:

- How do you feel?
- What was it like doing this exercise?
- How difficult was it for you to allow others to support your weight?
- In what ways do you struggle with allowing people to give you support in your life?
- How difficult was it to support others?
- Which did you worry about more: sitting on someone's lap, or someone sitting on yours?
- Did our success (or failure) surprise you? Why?

2nd Challenge: Human Ladder

Have members of the group hold the wooden dowels so they form an inclined ladder. Have a volunteer climb the ladder. As he or she clears the first rungs of the ladder, the people holding those can run around to the front and create additional rungs.

The climber can go up and down. The steps can be close or far apart, and the ladder can be as long or short as the group desires. Repeat the challenge with all of the members who want to try the climb.

Debrief

Have the group sit in a circle, then ask:

What was it like doing this exercise?

- How did you feel when you were off the ground and being supported by the group?
- What was it like when you were the one giving support to others?
- Which role was more difficult for you?
- What did you learn about yourself in doing this exercise?

3rd Challenge: Walk the Body

Individual volunteers fall backward as the group catches them and then swings them up so that the group is supporting the person parallel to the ground. (Falling back and being caught is easier than trying to lift someone off the ground.)

Then the group is to walk forward carefully for about a minute with the person in this position. Then they gently let the person back down to the ground. Repeat the challenge with as many group members as want to volunteer.

Debrief

Have the group sit in a circle, then ask:

- What was it like doing this exercise?
- How did you feel when you were off the ground and being supported by the group?
- What was it like when you were the one giving support?
- Which role was more difficult for you?
- What did you learn about yourself in doing this exercise?

Faith Link

Have volunteers read aloud the two Scriptures, then ask:

- What point is made in these two passages?
- What does this point have to do with the three exercises we just did?
- What does "bear one another's burdens" mean?
- How can we do that in real life?
- How can we do that within our group?
- What kinds of burdens do we have?
- How can we give support in these areas?
- When we do this for one another, how are we affected?

> **Watch the group carefully; be ready to assist if there is danger of the person being dropped.**

22

The Corporate
Connection

Supplies or Equipment:
3 milk crates or same-sized waste-baskets, 60–80 identical soft throwable balls or other objects that do not bounce much, masking tape, large sheet of paper, marker, stopwatch or clock with a second hand

Focus: *Group problem-solving*

Core Teaching: *As the body of Christ, all of us are needed. Each person is of sacred value and worth. As the apostle Paul reminds us, no one can say, "I am unimportant" and no one can say to another, "You are unimportant."*

Scripture: *1 Corinthians 12:13-21 (In the body, all parts are equally important and needed.)*

For in the one Spirit we were all baptized into one body—Jews or Greeks, slaves or free—and we were all made to drink of one Spirit. Indeed, the body does not consist of one member but of many. If the foot would say, "Because I am not a hand, I do not belong to the body," that would not make it any less a part of the body. And if the ear would say, "Because I am not an eye, I do not belong to the body," that would not make it any less a part of the body. If the whole body were an eye, where would the hearing be? If the whole body were hearing, where would the sense of smell be? But as it is, God arranged the members in the body, each one of them, as he chose. If all were a single member, where would the body be? As it is, there are many members, yet one body. The eye cannot say to the hand, "I have no need of you," nor again the head to the feet, "I have no need of you."

Group Size: 5–20 participants

Space: Indoors or outdoors; a cleared space at least 20 feet wide by 40 feet long. A wall at one end of this space is helpful but not necessary.

Preparation

❏ Arrange the 20 x 40 foot space as shown in the diagram on page 25.

The Challenge

Put the group in charge of producing a "product." Call it GIZMO or let the group choose a name for their product.

The goal of the group is to produce as many defect-free GIZMOS as possible per cycle. A cycle is two minutes. The group receives credit for one defect-free GIZMO for each object that they throw into the nearest milk crate, credit for three defect-free GIZMOS for each object that they throw into the middle crate, and credit for five defect-free GIZMOS for each object that they throw into the farthest crate.

CYCLE	CRATE 1	SUB-TOTAL	CRATE 3	SUB-TOTAL	CRATE 5	SUB-TOTAL	TOTAL
1							
2							
3							
4							
5							
6							

GIZMO COMPANY

Score per Crate

1 point—nearest
3 points—middle
5 points—farthest

The Process

The "company" has two distinct groups of workers: "throwers" and "retrievers." Throwers must stand behind the taped line and are the only ones who can score by throwing an object into the crate. Retrievers must stand on the other side of the line and can retrieve misses; but they cannot score, nor can a thrown object bounce off any part of their bodies and into a crate for a score. The group can choose any number of throwers or retrievers before the cycle begins; but once the cycle is in operation, no one can change jobs during that cycle.

Give the group members about five minutes to choose their roles and to ask any questions.

Start each cycle by stating, "Begin." After two minutes, call out, "Stop." Participants count the completed GIZMOS and tell the facilitator.

Write the total on a large sheet of paper prepared as shown. Announce the total; then give the company three minutes to decide how to change the process for the better.

Repeat the cycles as many times as necessary for the group members to discover that they will do better as they focus on the crates with a higher probability of success (closer rather than farther).

Variation: The facilitator may appoint a boss and direct the boss to make all decisions on company operations during the first two cycles, then allow for the workers to give input.

Debrief

Call the group together to sit in a circle, then ask:

- What were the barriers to success?
- What did you do that made you more successful?
- How did probability or statistics influence your decision-making?
- How did the style of leadership have an impact on the outcome?
- Who gave significant input?
- Why was it significant?

Faith Link

Read aloud 1 Corinthians 12:13-21, then ask:

- As Christians, what kinds of problems do we face?
- What did we learn today that we can apply to problems that we face in life?
- How can we "improve" our Christian faith?
- What does this have to do with our faith and Jesus' call for us to love our neighbor?
- What does it have to do with our Sunday school class or youth group?

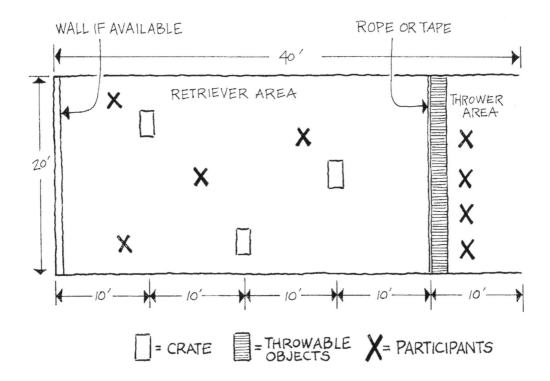

Count the Cost

Focus: *Discipleship, commitment, community of faith*

Core Teaching: *Discipleship is not easy. Jesus invites us to count the cost of discipleship, to consider what it takes to follow Christ.*

Supplies or equipment:

90-foot rope, 30 numbered spots (see below), masking tape or short rope, stopwatch

Scripture: *Luke 14:27-32 (You must carry the cross to be a disciple.)*

"Whoever does not carry the cross and follow me cannot be my disciple. For which of you, intending to build a tower, does not first sit down and estimate the cost, to see whether he has enough to complete it? Otherwise, when he has laid a foundation and is not able to finish, all who see it will begin to ridicule him, saying, 'This fellow began to build and was not able to finish.' Or what king, going out to wage war against another king, will not sit down first and consider whether he is able with ten thousand to oppose the one who comes against him with twenty thousand? If he cannot, then, while the other is still far away, he sends a delegation and asks for the terms of peace."

Group Size: 8–15

Space: Large area, outdoors or indoors

Preparation

❏ Using a permanent marker, consecutively number the spots from 1 to 30. (Use plastic lids such as those on a tennis-ball can or on cottage cheese or margarine containers. As an alternative you may cut the spots from construction paper.)

❏ With a 90-foot length of rope, establish a 15' x 30' rectangle on the gym floor or field.

❏ Inside the rectangle, place the numbered spots as illustrated (see next page). All even numbers should be on one side of the rectangle and all odd numbers on the other side. Zigzag the numbers up and down the rectangle. As you place the numbers, try to arrange them so that your odd/even and zigzag planning is not obvious. Note that numbers 1 and 30 are both located at one end of the rectangle, farthest away from the starting line.

When placing the spots, put them more than one step inside the boundary. This added distance forces the people touching the spots to step inside the boundary, not just reach over the edge. Thirty feet from the end of the rectangle, place a length of tape or rope to designate a starting line and to mark the planning area.

The Challenge

A militant group of nihilistic hackers have injected a VVV (very virulent virus) into the government's Socially Serious program. The group—highly trained computer experts—must wipe out the virus. Before them is the giant computer keyboard. To achieve the goal, they all must touch all 30 keys (spots) in sequence as quickly as possible.

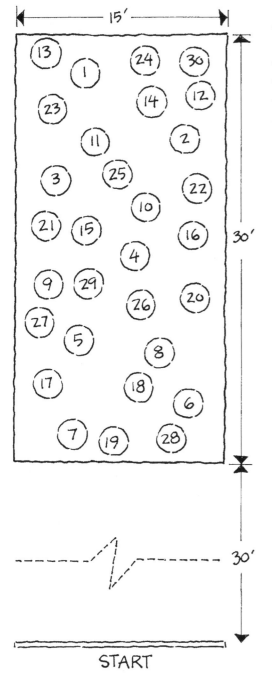

The Process

The entire group must begin and finish behind the start line. The stopwatch starts as soon as the first person steps over the line. The watch stops when the last person crosses back over the line.

When a person is inside the box, he or she must touch the keys only in order. If the person touches anything else (floor, ground) or goes the wrong way, she or he has to step out of the box, tag the next member of the group, and go to the back of the line. The new person will pick up with the next number.

Only one person may be on the keyboard at a time. That is, only one participant is allowed inside the boundary rope. If two are inside the rope simultaneously, that is a computer glitch. It adds penalty time to the score.

If anyone touches a number out of sequence, this infraction causes the computer to crash. A crash adds a penalty to the score.

Team members may use any part of the body to touch the keys.

The team may not study the keyboard between attempts. All planning must occur behind the line where the group starts each round. Any time the group or a player crosses this line is considered an attempt.

Tell the group that they have 30 minutes or five attempts, whichever comes first. If they use five attempts in 18 minutes, they're done; if they made only three attempts in 30 minutes, they're done.

Penalties: Ten seconds per infraction.

Debrief

- What was the exercise like for you?
- What difficulties did we experience?
- How did we overcome these difficulties?
- What was the secret to success in this exercise? (Did the group discover and use the odd/even, zigzag configuration of the keys?)
- What role did you play in the exercise?
- What different kinds of leadership did we need in this exercise?
- What role did counting play in the exercise?

Faith Link

Have a volunteer read aloud Luke 14:27-32, then ask:

- What is Jesus' point?
- Why might it be important to "count the cost" before following Jesus?
- What areas of our faith do you find the most demanding?
- What did you learn in this game that might help in aspects of our discipleship?
- How do we count the cost of our discipleship?

Diminishing Resources

Focus: *Community of faith, supporting one another, problem-solving*

Core Teaching: *God has given us much. But the most precious thing God has given us is one another. Christianity is a faith built with relationships. We are called into relationship with God and with one another. We need to value the contributions of other persons and to recognize that we are resources for one another.*

Scripture: *Numbers 11:11-17 (God gives Moses help with the people.)*

So Moses said to the LORD, "Why have you treated your servant so badly? Why have I not found favor in your sight, that you lay the burden of all this people on me? Did I conceive all this people? Did I give birth to them, that you should say to me, 'Carry them in your bosom, as a nurse carries a sucking child,' to the land that you promised on oath to their ancestors? Where am I to get meat to give to all this people? For they come weeping to me and say, 'Give us meat to eat!' I am not able to carry all this people alone, for they are too heavy for me. If this is the way you are going to treat me, put me to death at once—if I have found favor in your sight—and do not let me see my misery."

So the LORD said to Moses, "Gather for me seventy of the elders of Israel, whom you know to be the elders of the people and officers over them; bring them to the tent of meeting, and have them take their place there with you. I will come down and talk with you there; and I will take some of the spirit that is on you and put it on them; and they shall bear the burden of the people along with you so that you will not bear it all by yourself."

1 Kings 19:13-18 (God tells Elijah to appoint certain leaders.)

When Elijah heard it, he wrapped his face in his mantle and went out and stood at the entrance to the cave. Then there came a voice to him that said, "What are you doing here, Elijah?" He answered, "I have been very zealous for the LORD, the God of Hosts; for the Israelites have forsaken your covenant, thrown down your altars, and killed your prophets with the sword. I alone am left, and they are seeking my life, to take it away." Then the LORD said to him, "Go, return on your way to the wilderness of Damascus; when you arrive, you shall anoint Hazael as king over Aram. Also you shall anoint Jehu son of Nimshi as king over Israel; and you shall anoint Elisha son of Shaphat of Abelmeholah as prophet in your place. Whoever escapes from the sword of Hazael, Jehu shall kill; and whoever escapes from the sword of Jehu, Elisha shall kill. Yet I will leave seven thousand in Israel, all the knees that have not bowed to Baal, and every mouth that has not kissed him."

Group Size: 8–20 participants

Space: Indoors or outdoors

Preparation

❏ Have the group sit in a circle. Have the objects behind you where you can easily reach them. Ask the group to think of the resources available to them as a church or as a youth group. Have them mention as many as possible. Items might include the building, the church budget, the youth minister or pastor, the volunteers, parents, the Bible, and so on.

❏ After the group has mentioned as many resources as possible, begin to place the objects in the center of the circle and say:

❏ "Among the resources we have as a community of faith are the things we have just mentioned [*name a few of them*]. These objects represent all of our resources. Here is your challenge":

The Challenge

"Use the resources we have as a group (or church) to get the entire group off the floor. No one can be touching the floor, you must all be in physical contact with one another, and you must remain off the floor for a count of three (1, 2, 3). The only physical objects you may use are ourselves and the objects in the center of the circle."

The Process

Begin with the same number of objects as people in the group. After the participants have easily met the challenge, congratulate them. Then remove a couple of the objects as you say:

"Oops! The finance committee has just cut the budget for the coming year. Some of the resources we have been counting on are gone, but we're still expected to run the same program. Your task is the same."

Have the group members attempt the challenge again. This time it will be more difficult, but still fairly easy. Congratulate them when they have finished. Then pick up a couple more items from the floor and say:

"Sorry, I have some bad news. The church is growing and needs the space we have been meeting in for the new nursery. So we will just have to find another place to meet. But—you guessed it—our task is still the same."

Repeat the process over and over, mentioning resources that the group members listed and why they are being removed. Congratulate the participants for their successes. Continue until you get down to one item or until the group protests that the task cannot be done. Then say something like:

"You still have the resources you need to complete the challenge."

If they protest, you might want to say that they can successfully complete the challenge without any of the objects they have been using. Or you may want to withhold this information as they continue to problem-solve. Ask them if they want you to restate the challenge. When you repeat the challenge, stress the word *among.*

The Key

To solve this exercise the group has to realize that they don't need any of the physical objects in order to do the challenge—all they need is one another. All they have to do is hold hands, jump into the air while quickly saying "1, 2, 3"—and the challenge is done.

Most likely, however, the group will focus on the physical objects once they have been placed in front of them. This tendency will usually keep the participants from seeing the easiest and most obvious answer.

Debrief

Have the group sit in a circle around the objects, then ask:

- What was this exercise like for you?
- What was difficult about this exercise?
- How have you experienced something like this?
- How did we handle this loss as a group?
- How did we finally figure out the secret to this exercise?
- What did you feel when this happened?
- What did you learn from this exercise?

Faith Link

Read aloud Numbers 11:11-17, then ask:

- What was Moses' problem?
- Have you ever felt like that?
- What was God's solution to Moses' problem?
- How would that make a difference in Moses' work?
- What help has God given us?
- How can we draw help from one another in our life together?
- What did you learn from the exercise that relates to our discussion?

Read aloud 1 Kings 19:13-18, then ask:

- How many people did Elijah think were still faithful to God?
- How many did God say had not worshiped Baal and were still faithful?
- Why, do you think, could Elijah not see these resources?
- Have you ever felt alone and cut off as Elijah did?

The End of Your Rope

Supplies or Equipment:

one long rope, 3/4 to 1 inch in diameter, and preferably soft (for the final Pull-ups); 4 ropes (for The End of Your Rope)

Focus: *Coping, teamwork, supporting one another, problem-solving*

Core Teaching: *When we think we are at the end of our rope, there are always more options. God calls us beyond our limits. God challenges us to be open to new and exciting (if surprising) possibilities—and to be open to God's help in the midst of struggle.*

Scripture: *1 Kings 19:1-8 (The prophet Elijah comes to the end of his rope.)*

Ahab told Jezebel all that Elijah had done, and how he had killed all the prophets with the sword. Then Jezebel sent a messenger to Elijah, saying, "So may the gods do to me, and more also, if I do not make your life like the life of one of them by this time tomorrow." Then he was afraid; he got up and fled for his life, and came to Beer-sheba, which belongs to Judah; he left his servant there.

But he himself went a day's journey into the wilderness, and came and sat down under a solitary broom tree. He asked that he might die: "It is enough; now, O LORD, take away my life, for I am no better than my ancestors." Then he lay down under the broom tree and fell asleep. Suddenly an angel touched him and said to him, "Get up and eat." He looked, and there at his head was a cake baked on hot stones, and a jar of water. He ate and drank, and lay down again. The angel of the LORD came a second time, touched him, and said, "Get up and eat, otherwise the journey will be too much for you." He got up, and ate and drank; then he went in the strength of that food forty days and forty nights to Horeb the mount of God.

Group Size: pairs, groups of 4, groups of 8, groups of 12–15 people

Space: Outdoors or indoors; large area

Preparation

❏ Tie a rope around 3 or 4 trees or other objects at waist height.

❏ Tie a second rope to that rope so that one end dangles long enough for participants to use it, if they choose, to reach the third rope.

❏ Tie a third rope close by—not attached to either of the other ropes, but in reach of the second one when it is extended.

❏ Have a fourth rope with a sequence of knots in it available—but not attached to anything initially (see page 37). The diagram below will give you the idea.

❏ You will need one of these setups for each small group.

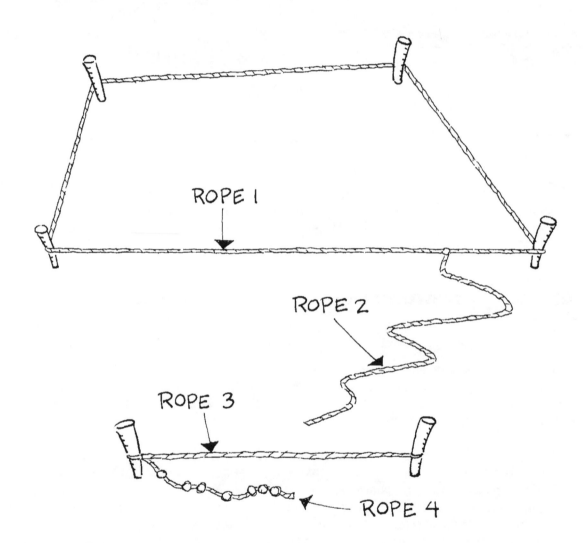

ROPE 1

ROPE 2

ROPE 3

ROPE 4

The Warm-up Challenges: Pull-ups

The challenge in each of these four activities is to help everyone stand up simultaneously. These experiences will also prepare the group for the final challenge: The End of Your Rope.

The Process for Pull-ups

Have the youth choose a partner and spread out. It is helpful to have partners close to the same weight. Adults may need to pair up with each other.

The pairs sit on the ground and then grab hands and simultaneously pull each other up. The picture will give you the basic idea.

Have the pairs choose another pair to form groups of 4 and pull themselves up in the same way.

Then the participants are to make groups of 8 and repeat the exercise.

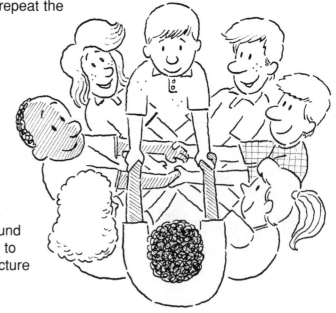

Finally, use the long, soft rope for pull-ups. Tie the rope in a circle. Have the group spread equally around the perimeter. Have everyone sit down and then try to stand simultaneously by pulling on the rope. The picture below will give you the idea.

The End of Your Rope

The Challenge: The End of Your Rope

The challenge is to find the treasure—by the Braille method.

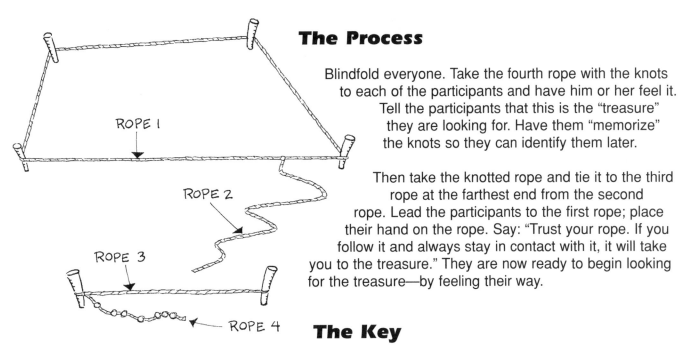

ROPE I

ROPE 2

ROPE 3

ROPE 4

The Process

Blindfold everyone. Take the fourth rope with the knots to each of the participants and have him or her feel it. Tell the participants that this is the "treasure" they are looking for. Have them "memorize" the knots so they can identify them later.

Then take the knotted rope and tie it to the third rope at the farthest end from the second rope. Lead the participants to the first rope; place their hand on the rope. Say: "Trust your rope. If you follow it and always stay in contact with it, it will take you to the treasure." They are now ready to begin looking for the treasure—by feeling their way.

The Key

In order to succeed, the participants must not only use Rope #1 (the one you place them on) but also Rope #2 (the one that will lead them to Rope #3) and Rope #3. If they are stuck and start going around in circles (they will), remind them of the instructions in the challenge. If the group gets really stuck, you can give some hints; for example, if they are at Rope #2, you could say, "The secret is in your hands—use it!"

Debrief

Have everyone sit in a circle, then ask:

- Were you successful? Why or why not?
- What were the problems or difficulties you encountered?
- How did you overcome these?
- Did you receive any help? (If so, what was this like for you?)
- What did you learn about us as a group?
- What did you learn about yourself?

Faith Link

Read aloud 1 Kings 19:1-8, then ask:

- Why did Elijah feel as if he was at the end of his rope?
- How have you reached the end of your rope in life?
- What enabled Elijah to go beyond that feeling?
- In what ways does God help us go beyond our own limits?
- What does this exercise have to do with being a Christian and our faith journey?
- What does this exercise have to do with our Sunday school class or youth group?

Escape From Auschwitz

Focus: *Responsibility for others, problem-solving, teamwork*

Core Teaching: *As a community of faith, we have responsibility to and for one another. We cannot go it alone. We are "our brother's keeper"—and our sister's.*

Scripture: *1 John 3:13-18 (Let us love in truth and action.)*

Do not be astonished, brothers and sisters, that the world hates you. We know that we have passed from death to life because we love one another. Whoever does not love abides in death. All who hate a brother or sister are murderers, and you know that murderers do not have eternal life abiding in them. We know love by this, that he laid down his life for us—and we ought to lay down our lives for one another. How does God's love abide in anyone who has the world's goods and sees a brother or sister in need and yet refuses help? Little children, let us love, not in word or speech, but in truth and action.

Supplies or Equipment:

Rope and a 1" by 12" by 8' board (Option 1) or yarn and chairs (Option 2)

Group Size: 8–20; extra adults monitoring for safety

Space: Outdoors (Option 1) or indoors (Option 2); small area

Preparation

Option 1: *outdoors (using a rope and the board)*
❑ Secure the rope tightly between two trees (or other stable, stationary objects) at a height of about 5 feet.
❑ Have the board lying on the ground inside the boundary of the "camp." Do not tell the group that they can use the board. Have them figure out that they can use the board.

Option 2: *indoors (using yarn, but no board)*
❑ Make two stacks of chairs about 12 to 15 feet apart.
❑ Tie the yarn to one stack and stretch it across to the other side, tying it off at the same height about 4 1/2 feet. The yarn should be tight.

The only tools the group is allowed to use to escape are one another's bodies. This second method is slower, more risky, and requires more adult spotting. It is also challenging and exciting in a positive sense.

The Challenge

The group is in a Nazi death camp and everyone is scheduled to be executed the next day. The camp is surrounded by an electrically charged fence (the rope in Option 1 or the yarn in Option 2). To touch the fence is to die. Guards with guns can see every section of the fence except this section.

The group must make it to safety by going over the fence without touching it. No one can go under or around the fence; everyone must go over it. The task is to get the entire group over the fence safely.

The Process

Require the group members to sit down and think through how they will accomplish the task. They may not use any objects other than their bodies or anything they can reach in the "camp." Do not specifically mention the board.

In the event that someone touches the fence, the group has to return the person to the ground and start over with him or her.

An important aspect of this exercise is physical and emotional safety. If at any point there is danger of injury, any youth or adult can call time out. Then ask the group to sit down; explain the danger, and have the group problem-solve for an alternative.

Debrief

It is possible that time will run out before everyone is over the fence. That's OK. The real goals of this exercise involve more than just succeeding. Ask:

• Were we successful? Why or why not?
• What were the problems or difficulties we encountered?
• How did we overcome these?
• What did you learn about us as a group?
• What did you learn about yourself?

Faith Link

Read aloud 1 John 3:13-18, then ask:

• How did it feel to be responsible for the safety of others?
• How did you feel when others held your safety in their hands?
• What does this exercise have to do with the Scripture we just read?
• What does this exercise have to do with being a Christian?
• What does this exercise have to do with our Sunday school class or youth group?

Eye of the Needle

Focus: *Setting priorities, reaching goals, letting go, cooperation*

Core Teaching: *Many things can weigh us down, encumber us, and keep us from reaching our goals and from being the people God has called us to be. Our wealth, our possessions, our attitudes, harmful habits—each of these can restrict us. In order to move on in our lives, in our discipleship, in our walk with God, we may have to lay aside some things.*

Scripture: *Matthew 19:16-26 (It is hard for persons encumbered with possessions to enter the kingdom of heaven.)*

Then someone came to him and said, "Teacher, what good deed must I do to have eternal life?" And he said to him, "Why do you ask me about what is good? There is only one who is good. If you wish to enter into life, keep the commandments." He said to him, "Which ones?" And Jesus said, "You shall not murder; You shall not commit adultery; You shall not steal; You shall not bear false witness; Honor your father and mother; also, You shall love your neighbor as yourself." The young man said to him, "I have kept all these; what do I still lack?" Jesus said to him, "If you wish to be perfect, go, sell your possessions, and give the money to the poor, and you will have treasure in heaven; then come, follow me." When the young man heard this word, he went away grieving, for he had many possessions. Then Jesus said to his disciples, "Truly I tell you, it will be hard for a rich person to enter the kingdom of heaven. Again I tell you, it is easier for a camel to go through the eye of a needle than for someone who is rich to enter the kingdom of God." When the disciples heard this, they were greatly astounded and said, "Then who can be saved?" But Jesus looked at them and said, "For mortals it is impossible, but for God all things are possible."

Hebrews 12:1 (Run the race with perseverance.)

Therefore, since we are surrounded by so great a cloud of witnesses, let us also lay aside every weight and the sin that clings so closely, and let us run with perseverance the race that is set before us.

Supplies or Equipment:

Old tire or inner tube, four ropes; several items of bulky clothing, heavy objects such as bricks or books (treasure). A laundry bag with 20 to 30 pounds of books would make an excellent treasure.

Group Size: 6–12 participants

Space: Outdoors

Preparation

☐ Using the four ropes, securely fasten an old tire or tire tube between two trees or other supports. If you use an inner tube, tape down the valve stem securely so that it cannot injure anyone. If at all possible, use a truck tire or truck tire tube. Fasten the tire or tube tightly so it cannot move or swing. The center of the tire should be about eye level.

The Challenge

Have the group sit in front of the tire. Create a story such as this:

We are on the *Titanic* and the ship has just hit an iceberg. The door is pinned shut and the only way out to safety is the porthole in front of us (the tire). Time is running out. We have a limited amount of time before the ship goes down. Our goal is for everyone to be saved, to make it out OK. We don't have any ladders or objects we can use to help us escape. All we have is one another.

The Process

Hand everyone a bulky article of clothing. Don't tell the participants that they have to put the items on. Just tell them it is cold outside. They will assume that wearing the clothing is part of the exercise. Then hand the participants the heavy objects (bricks, books, and so forth) or a box that is a bit too large to get through the opening in the tire. Say: "These objects are our treasures; they are very valuable. I'm sure you'll want to take these with you."

Make sure that one "treasure" is just slightly too large to fit through the porthole. That fact should not be obvious. It's better if the participants discover that the item doesn't fit as they are trying to get it through the hole.

Have the group members do the exercise. Let them know that they cannot use any objects to help them through the porthole, only one another. From time to time mention that the ship is rapidly sinking and that time is running out.

Debrief

Have the group sit in a circle near the porthole, then ask:

- What was it like doing this exercise?
- What was difficult about this exercise?
- Is there anything we could have done to make it easier or faster?
- Were we doing anything that made it harder than it needed to be?

If the participants don't figure out on their own that the extra clothing and the treasures were a problem, ask them:

- Why did you take the heavy, bulky clothing with you?

The group members may try to blame you and say that you told them to wear or take the clothing. If they do this, remind them of what you did say. No one told them they had to take the clothing. This was an assumption.

Do the same things with the heavy objects. Get the participants to explore why they felt they had to take things with them that obviously slowed them down and made it much more difficult to escape.

Faith Link

Have someone read aloud the two Scripture passages, then ask:

- What do these two passages have to do with the exercise we just did?
- In the game our goal was to get through the tire. What are our goals in life?
- What are our goals as people of God?
- In the game it was bulky clothing and heavy objects that slowed us down. What hinders us in real life?
- How real is this issue in your own life ("baggage" and "treasure" keeping you from achieving your goals, especially spiritual ones)?
- What did you learn in this exercise that you can use in your own faith journey and in your relationship with God?

Four Balls

Focus: *Communication, teamwork, cooperation, problem-solving, dealing with failure and frustration*

Core Teaching: *As the body of Christ, all of us are needed. Each person is of sacred value and worth. As the apostle Paul reminds us, no one can say "I am unimportant" and no one can say to another "you are unimportant."*

Scripture: *1 Corinthians 12:12-21 (In the body all parts are equally important and needed.)*

For just as the body is one and has many members, and all the members of the body, though many, are one body, so it is with Christ. For in the one Spirit we were all baptized into one body—Jews or Greeks, slaves or free—and we were all made to drink of one Spirit.

Indeed, the body does not consist of one member but of many. If the foot would say, "Because I am not a hand, I do not belong to the body," that would not make it any less a part of the body. And if the ear would say, "Because I am not an eye, I do not belong to the body," that would not make it any less a part of the body. If the whole body were an eye, where would the hearing be? If the whole body were hearing, where would the sense of smell be? But as it is, God arranged the members in the body, each one of them, as he chose. If all were a single member, where would the body be?

As it is, there are many members, yet one body. The eye cannot say to the hand, "I have no need of you," nor again the head to the feet, "I have no need of you."

Group Size: 8–15; if you have more than 15 people, create a second group.

Space: Indoors or outdoors; large enough for the small groups to form circles

Preparation: None

The Challenge

The challenge is to get all four balls simultaneously through a pattern—three times.

The Process

Have the group stand in a loose circle about a person-width between each one.

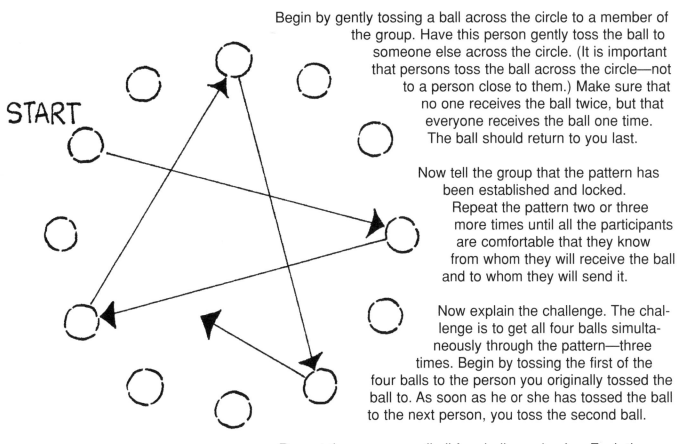

START

Begin by gently tossing a ball across the circle to a member of the group. Have this person gently toss the ball to someone else across the circle. (It is important that persons toss the ball across the circle—not to a person close to them.) Make sure that no one receives the ball twice, but that everyone receives the ball one time. The ball should return to you last.

Now tell the group that the pattern has been established and locked. Repeat the pattern two or three more times until all the participants are comfortable that they know from whom they will receive the ball and to whom they will send it.

Now explain the challenge. The challenge is to get all four balls simultaneously through the pattern—three times. Begin by tossing the first of the four balls to the person you originally tossed the ball to. As soon as he or she has tossed the ball to the next person, you toss the second ball.

Repeat the process until all four balls are in play. Each time there is a mistake—a collision, a ball missed, a ball hitting the floor, a ball to the wrong person—the group will immediately sit down and you will ask three questions:

- What went wrong?
- How do we fix it?
- Is everyone comfortable with this solution?

Only when the group members—as a group—are satisfied that they have answered the three questions can they stand up and try again.

Debrief

The goal of this exercise is gaining skills in communication, teamwork, cooperation, and problem-solving—not just succeeding. The more mistakes that are made, the more learning that will take place. Even failure to complete the task can mean successful learning. That is your real goal. Ask:

- Were we successful? Why or why not?
- What were the problems or difficulties we encountered?
- How did we overcome these difficulties?

- What did you learn about us as a group?
- What did you learn about yourself?

Faith Link

Read aloud 1 Corinthians 12:13-21, then ask:

- What is "the body" that Paul talks about in this passage?
- In the Scripture, how do the various parts of the body relate to one another?
- What do this example from the Scripture and the Four Balls activity have to do with our faith and our being a community?
- What do they have to do with our Sunday school class or youth group?

Four Balls

Islands

Focus: *Problem-solving, teamwork, individual gifts and abilities, leadership*

Core Teaching: *In our journey of faith we will face situations that we have not encountered before. In these situations we will need to rely on one another both for ideas and for help in solving the problem. Each of us has gifts and abilities that will help us and others. At times we use our gifts in leading. At other times we use our gifts in following.*

Scripture: *Romans 12:3-8 (We have gifts that differ, but we are members one of another.)*

For by the grace given to me I say to everyone among you not to think of yourself more highly than you ought to think, but to think with sober judgment, each according to the measure of faith that God has assigned. For as in one body we have many members, and not all the members have the same function, so we, who are many, are one body in Christ, and individually we are members one of another. We have gifts that differ according to the grace given to us: prophecy, in proportion to faith; ministry, in ministering; the teacher, in teaching; the exhorter, in exhortation; the giver, in generosity; the leader, in diligence; the compassionate, in cheerfulness.

Group Size: 8–10

Space: Outdoors; indoors if area is at least 20 feet across

Preparation

❏ Make the platforms out of 1/2 to 3/4 inch plywood with a 2 by 4 lumber base. On the larger platforms, it would be helpful to have an additional 2 by 4 brace in the middle.
❏ Place the three platforms on level ground so they are stable and do not rock.
❏ Put the smaller platform in the middle.
❏ Position the platforms so that the shortest distance between the platforms is about 7–8 feet—farther than the longer board can reach.
❏ Have your group members all stand on one of the large platforms.

The Challenge

Tell the group members they are marooned on a desert island in shark-infested waters. Their only resources are the two boards and one another. Their goal is to all travel safely to the far platform where they can be rescued. They may not touch the water (the ground or the floor). The sharks will eat anything that touches the water—people or boards.

The Process

If anyone or a board touches the water, dole out a consequence: Blindfold one

person, gag someone, or tie two persons together at the wrist.
Do not tell the group members how to use the boards. Let them figure out for themselves that they will need to use the two boards together in order to cross to the other islands. The drawing shows the key to the activity.

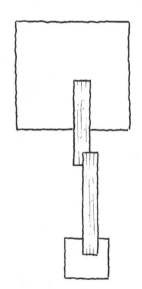

Debrief

Have the group sit in a circle near the platforms, then ask:

• What was the exercise like for you?
• What difficulties did we experience?
• How did we overcome these difficulties?
• What was the secret to success in this exercise?
• What role did you play in the exercise?
• What different kinds of leadership did we need in this exercise?

Faith Link

Have a volunteer read aloud Romans 12:3-8, then ask:

• What is Paul's point?
• How does this relate to what we just did?
• How did we work as a team in the exercise?
• What are your gifts that you can offer to the body?
• What gifts do others have that you find helpful?

NOTE:
If indoors, an alternative to the platforms would be to use collapsed tables as the islands. This setup decreases the difficulty of the activity, however.

Lifeline and Unseen Hands

Focus: *Trust, the Holy Spirit*

Core Teaching: *Our faith is like a lifeline that helps get us through dark times; the Holy Spirit is like unseen hands that guide us in those moments.*

Supplies or Equipment:

Yarn, blindfolds, trees, posts, or other objects to attach yarn to, 2–3 chairs or other obstacles

Scripture: *John 8:12 (Follow me, and you will not walk in darkness.)*

Again Jesus spoke to them, saying, "I am the light of the world. Whoever follows me will never walk in darkness but will have the light of life."

1 John 1:4-7 (God is light; walk in the light.)

We are writing these things so that our joy may be complete. This is the message we have heard from him and proclaim to you, that God is light and in him there is no darkness at all. If we say that we have fellowship with him while we are walking in darkness, we lie and do not do what is true; but if we walk in the light as he himself is in the light, we have fellowship with one another, and the blood of Jesus his Son cleanses us from all sin.

Group Size: 8–15 participants and at least 3 leaders; for more than 15 create additional small groups.

Space: Meeting area, separate space for the Lifeline course; size of the space needs to accommodate the group size

Preparation

☐ Set up a course with yarn. Tie it to trees and bushes if outside. Tie to door knobs, hinges, or various other types of obstacles if indoors.
☐ Make the course complicated. It can cross over itself several times, wrap around trees, and so forth. Use the whole skein of yarn—or two. Make the course 200–300 yards long.
☐ Designate a person to place the group on the Lifeline, a person to take them off, and one or more persons to watch for their safety while on the Lifeline.
☐ Designate persons to be the Unseen Hands at the obstacles on the course.
☐ Have the obstacles (chairs) ready to place for the Unseen Hands activity.

The Challenge

Say: "An important part of our faith journey is trust. In this session we will be doing three activities that call upon us to trust. In all three activities you will be blindfolded."

The Process

Trust Walk

Blindfold the group members. Have them hold hands or place their hands on the shoulders of the person in front of them as you lead them to the location of the Lifeline. With a large group, break into shorter lines and have additional leaders.

Go slowly. As you walk, tell the person behind you what you are coming to ("We're going down a little hill"; "There are three steps here"). Have him or her pass on the information to the next person in line.

Lifeline

Once your Trust Walk groups have arrived at the Lifeline course, have them stand without holding on to anyone. Take each person and put his or her hand on the Lifeline. Give these instructions:

> This is your Lifeline. There are three things you need to do:
>
> 1. Follow your Lifeline wherever it leads you.
>
> 2. Whatever you do, do not let go of your Lifeline—not even for a second, or you can get lost. Always maintain contact with your Lifeline. You will know when you come to the end.
>
> 3. Be careful. There may be obstacles along the path.

Start the participants at the beginning of the course. Do not guide them. Let them follow the yarn on their own. It is OK if they start going in reverse, stop, or otherwise mess up. These are things that happen to us in life.

Have an adult at the end of the course to stop the youth. Take a moment if needed to readjust blindfolds. Go immediately into Unseen Hands.

Unseen Hands

Repeat the Lifeline activity with these changes: Place two or three obstacles (a chair, for example) on the Lifeline course. Station one leader by each obstacle. Place the group members on the same course they were just on—but with a twist. This time start them in the opposite direction so that they are unfamiliar with the course.

As persons are about to collide with an obstacle, have the leader reach out and touch them gently—but say nothing. The instinctive reaction is to reach out and feel what is there. In this way they will discover the obstacle and go around it. The leader is not to say anything even if the group members attempt to speak to him or her.

Debrief

Have the group go back to its meeting location and debrief the three experiences. Ask:

Trust Walk

- What was the Trust Walk like for you?
- Was it easy or difficult?
- What made it difficult?
- How hard was it to trust in the exercise?
- Where is it hard to trust in life?

Lifeline

- What was the Lifeline experience like for you?
- Did you have any difficulties? If so, what were they?
- What enabled you to successfully complete the course?
- How did you know you were at the end?
- What kinds of things are our Lifeline in life? What do we hang on to? What do we use to guide us?
- What kinds of things form our Lifeline as Christians?
- How might God be a Lifeline in our lives? How might the Bible?

Unseen Hands

- What was the last exercise like for you?
- What happened when you were touched?
- How were you able to use the touch?
- Has something like that ever happened to you in real life?
- How does God guide us or warn us with unseen hands?
- How is this experience like the presence of the Holy Spirit in our lives?

Faith Link

Read aloud John 8:12 and 1 John 1:4-7, then ask:

- In today's world what kinds of "darkness" do people walk in?
- How can Jesus help us walk in that light?
- How is the Holy Spirit active in our lives?
- What do all of these exercises have to do with being a Christian? What do they have to do with our group?

Moses at the
Red Sea

Supplies or Equipment:
Masking tape, blindfolds, nearly the same number of wooden blocks as participants; the blocks can be a foot long, cut from boards either 1" by 8" or 2" by 8".

Focus: *Communication, teamwork, cooperation, problem-solving*

Core Teaching: *As a community of faith we sometimes come up against obstacles that seem insurmountable. Through trust in God and work on our part, we can pass through these obstacles—as people of faith have done throughout the ages.*

Scripture: *Exodus 14:10, 13-16, 21-22 (Moses gets God's help in crossing the Red Sea.)*

As Pharaoh drew near, the Israelites looked back, and there were the Egyptians advancing on them. In great fear the Israelites cried out to the LORD.... But Moses said to the people, "Do not be afraid, stand firm, and see the deliverance that the LORD will accomplish for you today; for the Egyptians whom you see today you shall never see again. The LORD will fight for you, and you have only to keep still."

Then the LORD said to Moses,... "But you lift up your staff, and stretch out your hand over the sea and divide it, that the Israelites may go into the sea on dry ground. ...

Then Moses stretched out his hand over the sea. The LORD drove the sea back by a strong east wind all night, and turned the sea into dry land; and the waters were divided. The Israelites went into the sea on dry ground, the waters forming a wall for them on their right and on their left.

Group Size: 6–12 persons per team

Space: About 20 to 30 feet of open space

Preparation

❏ Mark the starting points and finish lines for each group. Leave enough room for the groups to stand behind their starting boundary marker. There also needs to be room behind the marker for the group to stand as they finish.

❐ Place a special mark (masking tape) on three of the blocks given to each team.
❐ Distribute the wooden blocks. Each group is to have the same number as there are people in the group—minus 2. A group of 10, for example, will have 8 blocks.
❐ Designate a few "spies" (adults) to confiscate unattended blocks.

The Challenge

We are with Moses at the Red Sea. Pharaoh's army is just behind, so it is important that we get organized and get moving. This time, however, God does not part the waters. Instead, God—ever creative—has given us magic stepping stones. To fall into or even touch the Red Sea means death! The only way across the sea is by using the stepping stones (wooden blocks). Once the magic stones are in the river, you must keep in contact with them at all times; or you may lose them to Pharaoh's spies. Your challenge is to get the whole group safely to the other side using only the magic stepping stones.

Moses at the Red Sea

The Process

If a group member touches the ground, that person has to go back to the beginning point. The group will have to figure out how to rescue this person. Complicating this rescue is the fact that only three of the stepping stones can go backwards; they are the ones specially marked.

Pharaoh's spies are also in the sea. They can steal the magic stones when they are unattended. The spies cannot take away very many stepping stones without jeopardizing the game. However, losing one—or two—is a good lesson. Afterward, the threat of a spy is usually enough to make the group keep physical contact with their stepping stones.

In the event some persons are not taking the game seriously and they touch the floor, you can hand out consequences. Making the person be blindfolded (or gagged) for the remainder of the activity is usually enough.

Debrief

Have everyone sit in a circle. Ask:

- Were we successful? Why or why not?
- What were the problems or difficulties we encountered? How did we overcome these?
- What did you learn about us as a group? What did you learn about yourself?

Faith Link

Read aloud Exodus 14:10-22, then ask:

- What stands out in this Bible story?
- How do you think Moses felt when he faced the Red Sea?
- How did you feel when you faced your obstacle?
- What kinds of obstacles do you deal with today?
- What does this activity have to do with our faith?
- What does it have to do with our group?

Name Game and Do You Like Your Friends?

Focus: *Relationships*

Core Teaching: *The Christian faith is profoundly relational. God calls us into relationship with God and with people. It is important to know one anothers' names, to develop personal relationships, and to have fun together. In doing this we begin to learn how to "love one another."*

Scripture: *Luke 10:25-28 (God calls us to love one another.)*

Just then a lawyer stood up to test Jesus. "Teacher," he said, "what must I do to inherit eternal life?" He said to him, "What is written in the law? What do you read there?" He answered, "You shall love the Lord your God with all your heart, and with all your soul, and with all your strength, and with all your mind; and your neighbor as yourself." And he said to him, "You have given the right answer; do this, and you will live."

1 John 4:20-21 (We cannot love God without loving people.)

Those who say, "I love God," and hate their brothers or sisters, are liars; for those who do not love a brother or sister whom they have seen, cannot love God whom they have not seen. The commandment we have from him is this: those who love God must love their brothers and sisters also.

Group Size: Up to 20 in a group; a group of 12 to 15 is optimal

Space: Indoors or outdoors; classroom-size area

Preparation

❑ Set chairs in a circle.

The Challenge

The challenge is for group members—and leaders—to learn everyone else's name.

The Process

The Name Game

Introduce yourself and state one thing you like that begins with the same letter as your name.

For example, "I'm Walt and I really like watermelon." The next person has to repeat what the first person said, then add his or her own: "He's Walt, and he really likes watermelon. I'm Becca and I like baseball." The third person, repeats all that everyone has said and then adds his or her own. "He's Walt, and he likes watermelon; she's Becca and she likes baseball; I'm Jim and I like jelly beans."

Continue until everyone in the circle has had a turn. Then as the leader, you do the names for the whole group. Ask for volunteers to also do everyone's names. Then do a fruit basket turnover with everyone changing seats. See if anyone can still give the names of the entire group. Continue with the second game.

The Key

Go slowly enough so that everyone is anticipating the answer before it is given. This pace gives everyone a chance to practice the names and memorize them.

Do You Like Your Friends?

To play this game, everyone sits in a chair in a circle. There will be one extra person standing in the center of the circle without a chair. This person is going to attempt to get in one of the chairs.

He or she does this by walking up to someone in the circle and saying: "Do you like your friends?" There are two possible answers: yes or no. The "friends" are the persons sitting on his or her left and right. No matter what the answer is, the person who has been asked never moves. What everyone else does is determined by the answer.

If the person says, "Yes, I like my friends," the two friends freeze and do not move. Everyone else in the room does a fruit-basket turnover and finds a new seat at least two seats from where they were before. The person who asked the question will, of course, try to take one of the empty seats. Whoever is left will become "it" for the next round.

If the person says "No, I do not like my friends," the person calls the names of two other people in the group that he or she wants to have in their place. Then these four people—the two old friends and the two new friends—exchange seats. Of course, the person who asked the question will try to take one of the seats. Whoever is without a seat will be "it."

Debrief and Faith Link

Read aloud Luke 10:25-28 and 1 John 4:20-21. Then ask:

- Did you have fun today? What made it fun?
- Did you get to know anyone better today?
- What did you learn about others that you did not already know?
- What does this have to do with our faith and Jesus' call for us to "love our neighbor"?
- What does it have to do with our Sunday school class or youth group?

Owl Island

Focus: *Communication, cooperation, the common good*

Core Teaching: *God calls us to be a healing presence in the world. God has given us the gifts, the abilities needed, within the community of faith to do this. As we work together, it is important that we communicate accurately and effectively. Effective communication involves everyone. Each person plays an important role for the common good.*

Scripture: *1 Corinthians 12:4-9 (God gives each of us different gifts—for the common good.)*

Now there are varieties of gifts, but the same Spirit; and there are varieties of services, but the same Lord; and there are varieties of activities, but it is the same God who activates all of them in everyone. To each is given the manifestation of the Spirit for the common good. To one is given through the Spirit the utterance of wisdom, and to another the utterance of knowledge according to the same Spirit, to another faith by the same Spirit, to another gifts of healing by the one Spirit.

Group Size: 3–5 persons per team

Space: Indoors or outdoors; relatively large area or easily accessible separate rooms

Preparation

❏ Create a sample molecule, using the gumdrops and toothpicks. It can be relatively simple or more complex, depending upon your time and the experience level of the group.
❏ Divide the gum drops and toothpicks into bags. Be sure to have the exact number of the colors that correspond to the sample molecule. Then add extras.
❏ Optional: Use the masking tape to designate areas out of earshot and eyesight where each of the Bionic Persons can confer with their Geneticist and with their Biochemist.

The Challenge

A deadly, mutated form of the Ebola virus has broken out in the world. The fatality rate is

100%. The virus threatens to wipe out the human race. Millions have already died, and the virus is now in your country. There is only one hope. On a remote island in the middle of a sea of toxic wastes there is a person who has created an antivirus for Ebola. With this antivirus your team can save your country and the world.

One of your members—the Geneticist—must travel to the island and study the molecule so you will know how to build the antivirus. The problem is that the trip is one way only. The Geneticist can travel through the sea once, but would die if he or she tried to return with the information.

Another team member is Bionic and can survive many trips in the sea, but can only relay information—not having had any training in biochemistry. This person cannot leave the sea.

Your other team members are Biochemists. They can go to the edge of the sea, get the information from the Bionic Person, and then build the antivirus molecule.

The antivirus will work only if it is an exact duplicate of the original. One atom (gumdrop) or bond (toothpick) out of place and your country dies.

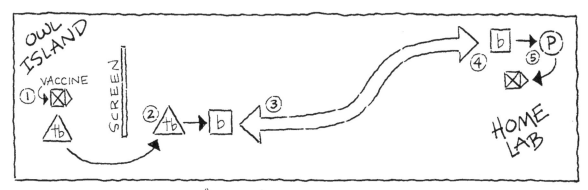

① THEORETICAL BIOCHEMIST ⟨tb⟩ STUDIES VACCINE.   ② ⟨tb⟩ RELAYS INFO ON HOW TO BUILD TO BIONICS ⟨b⟩   ③ ⟨b⟩ GOES BACK TO HOME LAB.

④ ⟨b⟩ RELAYS INFO TO PHARMACIST ⟨P⟩   ⑤ ⟨P⟩ RECONSTRUCTS VACCINE FOR COUNTRY.

The Process

The Geneticist has to go to the place where the antivirus molecule is located. This person views the molecule and will relay the information to the Bionic Person. The Geneticist cannot go beyond a designated point to relay the information to the Bionic Team Member. The Geneticist cannot see the molecule being built until the end of the game.

The Bionic Person never sees either the antivirus molecule (which the Geneticist sees) or the antivirus molecule (which the Biochemist is building). This person only hears the descriptions from the Geneticist and relays them to the Biochemist and listens to the questions asked by the Biochemist and relays them to the Geneticist. The Bionic Person cannot enter either location but can only go back and forth relaying information.

The Biochemist takes the information from the Bionic Person and tries to duplicate the molecule in the other room. If the Biochemist is uncertain about anything, he or she can ask questions through the Bionic Person. The Biochemist can only go to a designated point to talk to the Bionic Person.

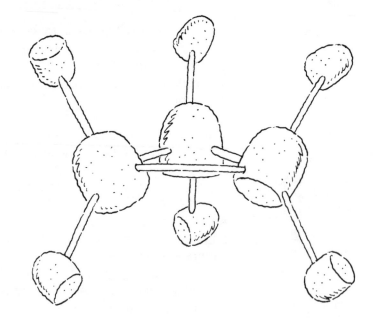

Debrief

The goal of this exercise is communication and teamwork—not just succeeding. The more mistakes made, the more learning that will take place. Even failure to complete the task can mean successful learning. That is your real goal. Ask:

- Were we successful? Why or why not?
- What were the problems or difficulties we encountered?
- How did we overcome these?
- What were some of the different abilities and skills needed to complete the task?
- What did you learn about us as a group?
- What did you learn about yourself?

Faith Link

Read aloud 1 Corinthians 12:4-9. Then ask:

- What kinds of problems do we face in the world today?
- What do you think God wants to do about these problems?
- Why do you think God created each of us with different abilities and gifts?
- Why is it important for us to work together to solve problems?
- What does all this have to do with being a Christian?
- What does it have to do with our Sunday school class or youth group?

River Crossing

Focus: *Problem-solving, teamwork*

Core Teaching: *In life, and in our faith, we will face situations in which it seems there are many possible answers, but only one that will help. Our ability to think—and our ability to work together—enable us to overcome many obstacles. At times, we will not be able to work out the solution to our problems in advance. Instead, we will need to work it out as we go.*

Scripture: *Ecclesiastes 4:9-12 (Two are better than one.)*

Two are better than one, because they have a good reward for their toil. For if they fall, one will lift up the other; but woe to one who is alone and falls and does not have another to help. Again, if two lie together, they keep warm; but how can one keep warm alone? And though one might prevail against another, two will withstand one. A threefold cord is not quickly broken.

Group Size: 6-10 persons per team

Space: Indoors or outdoors; at least classroom-size space

Preparation

❒ See the diagram.
❒ Lay out a course with only one real path across the river.
❒ Place the blocks so that the distance between them is just a little too long—except for certain blocks that form the hidden path.
❒ Design the spacing between the blocks so that on at least one occasion the team has to use a two-board combination to get to the next block.

The Challenge

The challenge is to get everyone across the river. No one is to touch the river (floor). If someone "falls in," he or she has to go back to the beginning, and the group will have to go back to rescue him or her.

The Process

Direct the group to the starting point. The group has to work together to find their way. If there are more than ten participants, you may want to start two groups at opposite ends Each group is to cross to the opposite side. In the middle they will be able to help one another by sharing boards—but let them figure that out for themselves!

The Key

The diagram gives an idea of how to do this challenge. There is only one path for making a successful crossing. On at least one occasion the team will need to use a two-board combination to bridge a gap. They can also pick up boards from behind and use them in front.

Debrief

- Were we successful? Why or why not?
- What were the problems or difficulties we encountered? How did we overcome these?
- How did the different teams relate when they met in the middle? (If we did this option.)
- What did you learn about us as a group?
- What did you learn about yourself?

Faith Link

Read aloud Ecclesiastes 4:7-12. Then ask:

- What is the main point of the Scripture we just read?
- What does that have to do with what we just did?
- What does it have to do with our Sunday school class or youth group?
- What does this exercise have to do with being a Christian?

The Shepherd's Voice

Focus: *Listening to God's voice in our lives*

Core Teaching: *For Christians, Jesus is our good shepherd—the one we trust, the one whose voice we listen to, the one who guides us to what is true and right. Listening to that voice and discerning it from others are keys to discipleship.*

Supplies or Equipment:

Blindfolds, yarn, chairs and other obstacles; bungee cords and hanging objects (optional)

Scripture: *John 10:6-18 (The Good Shepherd)*

Jesus used this figure of speech with them, but they did not understand what he was saying to them.

So again Jesus said to them, "Very truly, I tell you, I am the gate for the sheep. All who came before me are thieves and bandits; but the sheep did not listen to them. I am the gate. Whoever enters by me will be saved, and will come in and go out and find pasture. The thief comes only to steal and kill and destroy. I came that they may have life, and have it abundantly.

"I am the good shepherd. The good shepherd lays down his life for the sheep. The hired hand, who is not the shepherd and does not own the sheep, sees the wolf coming and leaves the sheep and runs away—and the wolf snatches them and scatters them. The hired hand runs away because a hired hand does not care for the sheep. I am the good shepherd. I know my own and my own know me, just as the Father knows me and I know the Father. And I lay down my life for the sheep. I have other sheep that do not belong to this fold. I must bring them also, and they will listen to my voice. So there will be one flock, one shepherd. For this reason the Father loves me, because I lay down my life in order to take it up again. No one takes it from me, but I lay it down of my own accord. I have power to lay it down, and I have power to take it up again. I have received this command from my Father."

Psalm 23 (The LORD is my shepherd.)

The LORD is my shepherd, I shall not want. He makes me lie down in green pastures; he leads me beside still waters; he restores my soul. He leads me in right paths for his name's sake. Even though I walk through the darkest valley, I fear no evil; for you are with me; your rod and your staff—they comfort me. You prepare a table before me in the presence of my enemies; you anoint my head with oil; my cup overflows. Surely goodness and mercy shall follow me all the days of my life, and I shall dwell in the house of the LORD my whole life long.

Group Size: 6–10

Space: Outdoors or indoors

Preparation

❐ Set up a course outside or clear a path in a room lengthwise from wall to wall.
❐ Place several obstacles (chairs, for example) in the center of the path.
❐ Optional: Use yarn, bungee chords, hanging objects, and so forth to give a 3D-effect to the obstacle course.

The Challenge

The challenge is for the Lost Lamb to determine which voice to follow to safety.

One person is the Lost Lamb; another, the Shepherd; and a third, the Wolf. The rest of the group is Noise.

The Noise group is to talk, chat, make noise, but they are not deliberately to try to lead the Lamb off the course.

The Wolf, on the other hand, is to try to lead the Lamb astray. If the Wolf can successfully confuse the Lamb enough so that the Lamb walks to where the Wolf is, the Wolf has "lunch."

The Shepherd is to guide the Lamb safely to the other side of the room without hitting any of the obstacles.

The Process

Blindfold the Lamb and have this person stand at one end of the room. Have the other group members (Shepherd, Noise, and Wolf) stand at the other end of the room. The Shepherd is to give the Lamb directions. The Wolf is to give false instructions or try to cover up the voice of the Shepherd.

The Shepherd can move anywhere in the room to give instructions but cannot get closer than six feet and must keep his or her voice at a normal conversational level.

The Wolf has to remain on the opposite wall but can speak loudly.

Those playing the part of Noise can travel anywhere, but they can only speak in a normal talking voice. In addition, Noise cannot speak directly to the Lamb. Their statements and conversation must be about other topics.

Do this activity two ways:

• The first time have the group member who knows the Lamb the least be the Shepherd. Allow the blindfolded Lamb to hear the Shepherd's voice clearly. Then begin.
• The second time have someone the Lamb knows be the Shepherd. Allow the blindfolded Lamb to hear the Shepherd's voice clearly. Then begin.

Repeat the exercise as time allows, switching roles so more persons can experience being the Lamb, Shepherd, or Wolf.

Debrief

Have the group sit in a circle; ask the blindfolded volunteer:

- What was that like for you?
- What made the exercise difficult?
- What enabled you to cross the room safely?
- How difficult was it to trust the voice of the Shepherd?
- How distracting were the other voices?
- Was the Wolf able to trick you in any way?

Faith Link

Have volunteers read aloud the two Scriptures, then ask:

- What are the passages trying to say by speaking of Jesus/God as a shepherd?
- What insights do these passages give you into the nature of God/Jesus?
- What insights does the exercise give you into hearing God's voice in our lives?
- Have you ever had an experience that you would call "hearing God's voice" in your own life? If so, please tell us about it.
- If God were to try to speak to you in some way, how would you recognize the voice as God's?
- What is the key to being able to sort out God's voice from other voices around us?
- What kinds of things in your life do you experience as "noise"?
- What kinds of things in your life do you experience as "the wolf"?

Space  Web

Supplies or Equipment:

Ropes, bungee cords, blindfolds, objects such as tennis balls or wads of paper ("alien food")

Focus: *Caring for one another*

Core Teaching: *For Christians, even in the midst of other activities, caring for one another takes precedence.*

Scripture: *Luke 10:25-28 (Love God with your whole being.)*

Just then a lawyer stood up to test Jesus. "Teacher," he said, "what must I do to inherit eternal life?" He said to him, "What is written in the law? What do you read there?" He answered, "You shall love the Lord your God with all your heart, and with all your soul, and with all your strength, and with all your mind; and your neighbor as yourself." And he said to him, "You have given the right answer; do this, and you will live."

1 John 4:20-21 (We do not love God unless we love people also)

Those who say, "I love God," and hate their brothers or sisters, are liars; for those who do not love a brother or sister whom they have seen, cannot love God whom they have not seen. The commandment we have from him is this: those who love God must love their brothers and sisters also.

Group Size: 8–20; with more participants, break into smaller groups

Space: Outdoors or indoors; large enough for the group to move freely through the web, but space also for them to plan before entering the web

Preparation

❑ Layout a perimeter rope to give the web an outside boundary.
❑ Build the web by connecting ropes and bungees; use trees or stacks of chairs as anchor points.
❑ Build the web horizontally about 14 inches off the ground.
❑ Make the web multi-dimensional by connecting other ropes or bungee chords at angles.
❑ Next place the "alien food" (one for each person doing the exercise) within the web.
❑ Use extra blindfolds to designate entrance and exit locations.
❑ Have the group walk around the web for a couple of minutes and examine it. Then have them sit in a circle both to hear the information about the challenges and to plan how they will accomplish them.

First Challenge

Welcome to the space web. This is a two-level challenge. I will give you the first challenge. Your group will have time to talk and come up with a solution. Once you have your plan, I will give you the second challenge. Here is the first challenge:

The space web is three-dimensional. You can see pieces of "alien food" within the web. Your challenge is to figure out how to get all of the food (the objects in the web) out of the web safely with no

more than three touches. A touch is any contact with either the web or a piece of alien food. You have to go over the horizontal part of the web and under any other part. Everyone must be in the web at one time. You have to enter the web at one end and exit at the other end.

The Process

Give the group a few minutes to problem solve. The answer is that the alien can only sense one touch at a time. If the group members all pick up their pieces at the same time, it only counts as one touch.

Do not give them the answer. Let them problem solve. But let them know that you can answer any questions and you can let them know if something is allowed or not.

After they have uncovered the "secret," have them plan how they will do the challenge:

Who will get each piece of the alien food?
How will they get into the web and out?
How will they handle any difficulties?
How will they coordinate the pick up of the alien food?
And so on.

Second Challenge

Once the group has solved the first challenge, has a plan, and is ready to enter the web, stop them and give them the second challenge:

Tell the group that their challenge remains the same (to safely remove the alien food from the web), but that they now need to make allowances for the handicaps of some of their members. They have to care for those members who have special needs or limits. They are no longer limited to three touches. Their new challenge is to have as few touches as possible.

The Process

Blindfold one person. Use another blindfold to tie two of the group together at the ankle. Tie a third blindfold over the mouth of the person who was the most vocal during the first challenge. Tie two members together at the wrists.

Have them—as a group—agree on the smallest number of touches within which they think they can now do the exercise

Let the group begin the challenge.

Debrief

Have the group sit in the circle, and then ask the following questions. Be sure to invite several youth to answer each question. Be supportive and non-judgmental as they answer.

- How do you feel right now?
- How did we do in dealing with our two challenges? Why do you think this is true?
- What was the real challenge in this activity?
- How does this relate to our real lives? Where do we face the same problem?
- How does the second experience relate to our Sunday school class?
- How does it relate to being a Christian?
- What did you learn during this exercise about us as a group?
- What did you learn about yourself?

Faith Link

Read aloud the passages from Luke and First John, then ask:

- What is the point of today's two Scripture lessons?
- Why do you think the Bible stresses love so much?
- What does it really mean to love?
- What does love have to do with what we did today?
- What examples did you see of love in the exercise?
- How might we have loved more in the exercise?
- How can we love more in our real lives?
- What did you learn about the role of love in faith?

Spider

Focus: *Teamwork, problem-solving, leadership*

<table>
<tr><td>

Supplies or Equipment:

Yarn, vertical supports for holding the web (can be trees or plastic pipes, for example)

</td></tr>
</table>

Core Teaching: *All of us have gifts and abilities. There is a time when we need to lead, and a time when we need to be led; a time to support others, and a time to be supported. There is a time and a purpose for everything.*

Scripture: *Ecclesiastes 3:1-8 (There is a time for everything.)*

For everything there is a season, and a time for every matter under heaven: a time to be born, and a time to die; a time to plant, and a time to pluck up what is planted; a time to kill, and a time to heal; a time to break down, and a time to build up; a time to weep, and a time to laugh; a time to mourn, and a time to dance; a time to throw away stones, and a time to gather stones together; a time to embrace, and a time to refrain from embracing; a time to seek, and a time to lose; a time to keep, and a time to throw away; a time to tear, and a time to sew; a time to keep silence, and a time to speak; a time to love, and a time to hate; a time for war, and a time for peace.

Group Size: 8–12 persons

Space: Outdoors or indoors

Preparation

❑ Use trees, plastic pipes, or other vertical supports to construct a frame for the web about 10 feet wide and 7 feet high.
❑ String the yarn back and forth to create a web.
❑ Be sure to leave holes large enough for persons to pass through. You will need one hole per person. On occasion—if the group is large—they may reuse a limited number of holes.

The Challenge

The challenge for the group is to get through the web. They cannot go under, over, or around the web. The group must go through the web. The group cannot use any object except their bodies. Once someone has used an opening, no one else can use it.

The Process

The group needs to think about who goes first and who goes last, about who goes low and who goes high.

Make sure to attend to safety. No one should be in any physical danger at any time.

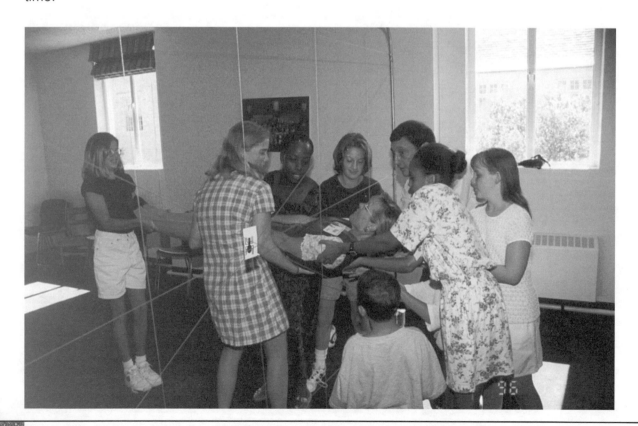

Spider Web

Debrief

Have the group sit in a circle by the web. Ask:

* Were we successful? Why or why not?
* What were the problems or difficulties we encountered? How did we overcome these?
* What did you learn about us as a group?
* What did you learn about yourself?

Faith Link

Read aloud Ecclesiastes 3:1-8. Then ask:

* Is there a time to lead in the activity we just did? When was it?
* Is there a time to follow? When?
* Which was easier for you? Which was harder?
* Which is the more important in the exercise? in life? in our faith?
* What does this exercise have to do with our Sunday school class or youth group?
* What does this exercise have to do with being a Christian?

Squares

Focus: *Giving*

Core Teaching: *The Christian faith emphasizes giving rather than taking.*

Scripture: *Mark 9:33-37 (Whoever would be greatest must be servant of all.)*

Then they came to Capernaum; and when he was in the house he asked them, "What were you arguing about on the way?" But they were silent, for on the way they had argued with one another who was the greatest. He sat down, called the twelve, and said to them, "Whoever wants to be first must be last of all and servant of all." Then he took a little child and put it among them; and taking it in his arms, he said to them, "Whoever welcomes one such child in my name welcomes me, and whoever welcomes me welcomes not me but the one who sent me."

John 13:3-15 (Jesus washes the feet of the disciples)

Jesus, knowing that the Father had given all things into his hands, and that he had come from God and was going to God, got up from the table, took off his outer robe, and tied a towel around himself. Then he poured water into a basin and began to wash the disciples' feet and to wipe them with the towel that was tied around him. He came to Simon Peter, who said to him, "Lord, are you going to wash my feet?" Jesus answered, "You do not know now what I am doing, but later you will understand." Peter said to him, "You will never wash my feet." Jesus answered, "Unless I wash you, you have no share with me." Simon Peter said to him, "Lord, not my feet only but also my hands and my head!" Jesus said to him, "One who has bathed does not need to wash, except for the feet, but is entirely clean. And you are clean, though not all of you." For he knew who was to betray him; for this reason he said, "Not all of you are clean."

After he had washed their feet, had put on his robe, and had returned to the table, he said to them, "Do you know what I have done to you? You call me Teacher and Lord—and you are right, for that is what I am. So if I, your Lord and Teacher, have washed your feet, you also ought to wash one another's feet. For I have set you an example, that you also should do as I have done to you."

Group Size: 5–9 per team; for 10 or more create additional teams

Space: Indoors; classroom-size area at least

Preparation

❑ Cut out 5 cardboard squares, each exactly 6 inches by 6 inches.
❑ Place the squares in a row and mark them as in the diagram, penciling the letters lightly so you can erase them.
❑ Draw the lines so that, when the pieces are cut out, those marked A will be exactly the same size, all pieces marked C the same size, and so on.
❑ Cut each square along the lines to make the puzzle pieces.
❑ Label the five envelopes 1, 2, 3, 4, and 5. Distribute the cardboard pieces into the five envelopes as follows:

Envelope 1 has pieces I, H, E
Envelope 2 has A, A, A, C
Envelope 3 has A, J
Envelope 4 has D, F
Envelope 5 has G, B, F, C

Erase the penciled letter from each piece and write, instead, the number of its envelope. This step makes it easy to return the pieces to the proper envelope, for subsequent use, after a group has completed the task.

The Challenge

When properly arranged, these pieces will form five squares of equal size. Several combinations are possible that will form one or two squares, but only one combination will form all five squares, each 6 inches by 6 inches. The challenge for the team is to put them all together.

Issue these rules:

You may not communicate with one anotherùverbally or nonverbally.
You must each put together a square.
You may not take a square piece from another individual unless he or she offers it.
The task is complete when the group puts together all five squares.
Pieces may not be set in the middle for just anyone to take. They must be given to a specific individual.

The Process

Give five of the participants in each group an envelope. Instruct the participants who do not have envelopes to be observers. They are to watch and make mental notes about the group's interaction.

Tell the participants to complete the square-building task as quickly as possible. Do not give a specific time limit, but periodically tell them to hurry.

The Key
No one may take, but anyone may give—if he or she is willing. The sets of squares are such

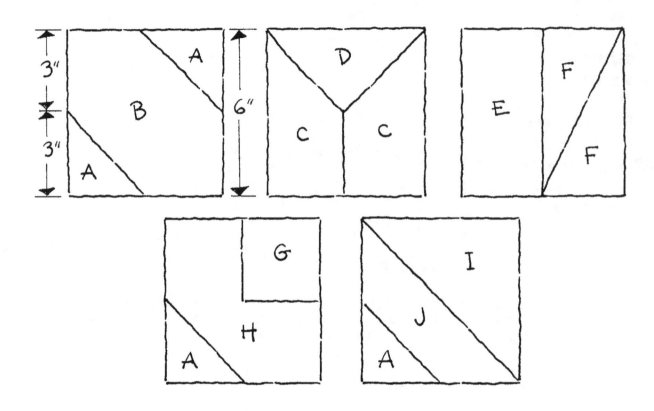

that one person may, after completing his or her square, need to break that square up in order for all the members' squares to come together.

Sometimes all of the participants hand their pieces over to one person to put together only to find that they could actually have put the squares together better themselves. Each of these scenarios may cause frustration, but that is part of the activity. Human tendency is to take rather than to give.

Debrief

Have the team sit in a circle. Ask the participants:

- How did you feel as you worked on this project? frustrated? anxious? Explain.
- Could you have done anything different to complete the task more quickly?

Have each designated observer give his or her observations. Then ask the group:

- What was the key to solving the problem?
- Who initially was willing to give away his or her pieces?

Faith Link

Read aloud Mark 9:33-37 and John 13:3-15, then ask:

- What does Jesus call us to do?
- How does this exercise relate to the Scripture passages?
- Is the giving (or lack of giving) that you displayed in this exercise in any way typical of yourself in other situations?
- As a result of this exercise, what is one thing you learned about yourself?
- As you think about being a follower of Jesus Christ, what are you willing to give
  - to the church?
  - to the youth group?
  - to your relationships (with friends, family and church family)?
  - to persons in need?

3D Minefield

Focus: *Responsibility, caring for others*

Core Teaching: *We are our brother's and sister's keeper. We can—and should—help one another through the dangers of life. We can also help guide one another through difficulties encountered on our faith journey.*

Scripture: *Ecclesiastes 4:9-12 (Two are better than one.)*

Two are better than one … For if they fall, one will lift up the other; but woe to one who is alone and falls and does not have another to help. … And though one might prevail against another, two will withstand one. A threefold cord is not quickly broken.

Group size: 6–50, depending upon size of the "mine field"

Space: Indoors or outdoors; large area

Preparation

❑ Create a three-dimensional mine field. Use rope or string and bungee chords strung across the area at weird angles to give it a 3-D effect. Tie these to trees, doorknobs, whatever is handy. Make the area complicated and intense.

❑ Clutter the area with objects on the floor or ground and hanging down from the ceiling or trees. All of the objects symbolize dangers— mines, booby traps, snares, things that can hurt and kill.

❑ Designate various starting and ending points.

❑ Lead your group to the area.

Supplies or Equipment:
Rope or string, tape, bungee chords, miscellaneous objects, blindfolds

The Challenge

The goal of this activity is for group members to successfully guide one another through the 3D minefield. "Success" means traveling safely across the area without coming in contact with any of the "mines" and being "injured." The fact that many other people will be in the minefield at the same time will complicate the task. They become added obstacles to avoid, added distractions, and an added degree of difficulty.

The Process

Have everyone pair off and blindfold one partner. Have the sighted one lead the blindfolded person around the perimeter of the course a couple of times and enter at new angle. The goal is to confuse the blindfolded partner so that he or she cannot memorize the path across the minefield. The various pairs will be entering the course at different points and traveling in opposite directions.

Once the journey has begun, the sighted partner is not to use his or her hands—only the voice. Challenge the pairs to go slowly. The goal is a safe and successful transit—not speed.

After the pair has finished, have them trade roles and do the exercise again.

Debrief

Have the group sit in the circle. Ask the following questions. Invite more than one youth to answer each question. Be supportive and non-judgmental as the youth answer.

- What was that like for you being blind-folded and led? How did it feel?
- What was it like listening to someone else's guidance?
- What did your guide do that was helpful?
- What did you learn about yourself?
- What was it like for you to be a guide?
- What were the keys to helping someone safely through the minefield?
- What made this journey harder?
- What did you learn about yourself?

Faith Link

- What obstacles are we likely to encounter in our life and faith journeys during the next few years?
- How can we help guide one another through these obstacles?
- What have you learned in this exercise that you might be able to apply to the future in both our life and our faith journey?

Read aloud Ecclesiastes 4:7-12. Ask:

- What is the point of the passage? Is it true?
- How can we as a church, a class, youth group, or friends who share beliefs and values lift up one another in the months and years to come?
- What specific dangers do you see that we might face?
- How can we help one another through these "minefields"?
- What do you need from one another to make it safely through this journey?

Toxic Waste

Focus: *Teamwork, problem solving, the common good, responsibility*

Core Teaching: *There are some things that we simply cannot do by ourselves. There are times when it is to our benefit to work as a part of a team for the common good. God gave us minds to think and dominion over creation so that we can use our natural resources to improve our world. As a team, we can draw upon everyone's creative ideas and physical abilities.*

Scripture: *Genesis 1:26-31a (God charges humankind to care for creation.)*

Then God said, "Let us make humankind in our image, according to our likeness; and let them have dominion over the fish of the sea, and over the birds of the air, and over the cattle, and over all the wild animals of the earth, and over every creeping thing that creeps upon the earth."

So God created humankind in his image,
in the image of God he created them;
male and female he created them.

God blessed them, and God said to them, "Be fruitful and multiply, and fill the earth and subdue it; and have dominion over the fish of the sea and over the birds of the air and over every living thing that moves upon the earth." God said, "See, I have given you every plant yielding seed that is upon the face of all the earth, and every tree with seed in its fruit; you shall have them for food. And to every beast of the earth, and to every bird of the air, and to everything that creeps on the earth, everything that has the breath of life, I have given every green plant for food." And it was so. God saw everything that he had made, and indeed, it was very good.

Group Size: 5–7 people per set up

Space: Outdoors or indoors, 30-foot-diameter space

Preparation

❏ Lay out a circle about 30 feet in diameter with rope or yarn. This is the boundary that the group cannot cross.
❏ Then place a #10 can about 1/3 full of water or small balls in the center.

□ Put the follow-
ing items out-
side the circle:
a bicycle inner
tube (cut so
that is lays out
like a snake),
three pieces of
rope about 20
feet long, and
one section of
rope about 40
feet long.

□ Do this setup
for each group
of 5–7 people.

The Challenge

The objective is to
retrieve the toxic
waste (water, balls) from the circle without spilling it (toxic spill—not good!), and
thereby save the world (yea!). The group has to figure out how to use their
resources (inner tube and ropes) to do this. Create a scenario: a nuclear
accident or toxic spill has happened … and so on. (A brief story to set up
the exercise always helps!)

The Process

Give the team the
ropes and inner
tube. Have them plan
how they will use their
resources to do the job.
Then they can try out
their ideas.

If they figure out the solution quickly, add a twist.
Challenge the group to
safely transfer the toxic
waste into a second
container (for ship-
ping to a toxic-
waste dump, of
course!).

The Key

The picture shows the solution. But … they need to figure it out for themselves (problem #1) and then work as a team to safely extract the toxic
substance (problem #2).

Debrief

The goal of this exercise is problem-solving and teamwork—not just succeeding. Even failure to complete the task can mean successful learning. That is your real goal. Ask:

- Were we successful? Why or why not?
- What were the problems or difficulties we encountered?
- How did we overcome these?
- What did you learn about us as a group?
- What did you learn about yourself?

Faith Link

Read aloud Genesis 1:26-31. Then ask:

- What responsibility has God given us over creation?
- What resources has God given us that will help us do this?
- What does this experience have to do with the Scripture we just read?
- What does this exercise have to do with being a Christian?
- What does this exercise have to do with our Sunday school class or youth group?

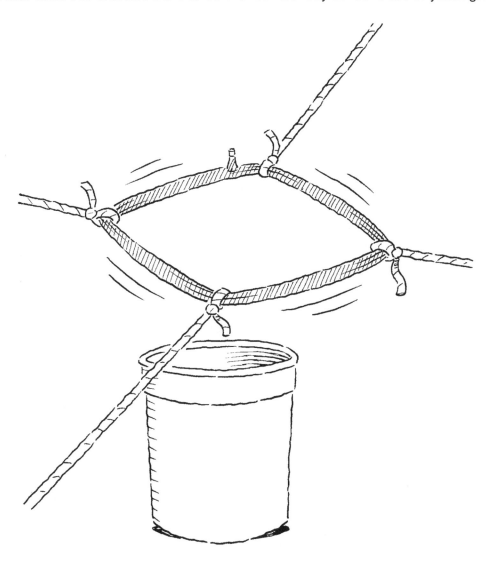

Trust Exercises

Focus: *Building trust, confidence, and community*

Core Teaching: *As Christians we are called to faith. One of the primary elements of faith is trust. We are called to trust God and to trust others— something that is not always easy to do. One purpose of these activities is to have the group begin to trust one another with their physical and emotional safety.*

Scripture: *Genesis 12:1-5 (Abraham trusts God.)*

Now the LORD said to Abram, "Go from your country and your kindred and your father's house to the land that I will show you. I will make of you a great nation, and I will bless you, and make your name great, so that you will be a blessing. ... So Abram went, as the LORD had told him; and Lot went with him. Abram was seventy-five years old when he departed from Haran. Abram took his wife Sarai and his brother's son Lot, and all the possessions that they had gathered. ... and they set forth to go to the land of Canaan.

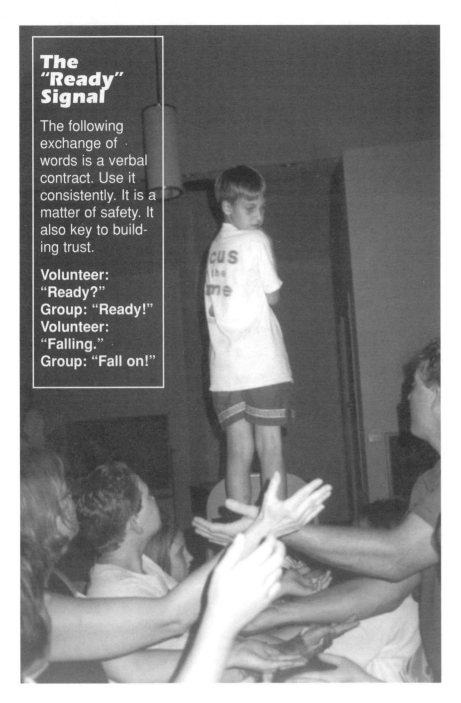

The "Ready" Signal

The following exchange of words is a verbal contract. Use it consistently. It is a matter of safety. It also key to building trust.

Volunteer: "Ready?"
Group: "Ready!"
Volunteer: "Falling."
Group: "Fall on!"

Romans 4:4-5 (Abraham's trust is an example for us.)

For what does the scripture say? "Abraham trusted God, and it was reckoned to him as righteousness." Now to one who works, wages are not reckoned as a gift but as something due. But to one who without works trusts him who justifies the ungodly, such trust is reckoned as righteousness.

Group Size: About 8; at least one adult in each group

Space: Indoors

Preparation

❑ Stack chairs or provide a table and chair for each group for the Single Chair Drop.
❑ Think safety first: Make sure the platform is stable.

First Challenge: Willow in the Wind

The group stands and forms a tight circle with their hands in front—palms flat—near their chests. A volunteer steps to the center, closes his or her eyes, folds his or her arms across the chest, and stands rigid.

All of these exercises are "challenge by choice." No one is forced to go.

At the "Ready" signal, the person falls backward about 6 inches to be caught by the group.

The group then gently passes the volunteer around the circle—like a willow tree being gently blown in the wind.

The volunteer's feet never move. The volunteer does not bent at the knees or waist. The volunteer pivots only at the ankles. The rest of the body is rigid. The picture should give you the idea.

The group should always have several members supporting the volunteer. They can lightly place their hands on the shoulders.

The group gently passes the volunteer around and back and forth for about 30 seconds.

Then they return the person to the center upright, and she or he can open his or her eyes.

Repeat the challenge with each person who is willing, including the adults.

Second Challenge: Log Toss

The group forms two semicircles—one in front of the volunteer and one behind.

The volunteer assumes the same stance as in the first challenge: eyes closed, arms crossed on chest, body rigid, pivoting from the ankles.

The volunteer initiates the Ready signal and then falls back about six inches.

The group behind gently catches and then sends the volunteer forward to be caught by the group in front (about 6 inches forward).

The groups pass the volunteer back and forth, each time increasing the distance of the fall to about two feet.

Repeat the process with each person in the group who is willing to go—including adults.

Third Challenge: Falling Leaf

The volunteer assumes the basic stance: eyes closed, arms crossed on chest, body rigid.

Behind the volunteer, the group forms two lines, facing each other, hands outstretched.

The volunteer initiates the Ready signal and then falls back. The group catches the volunteer and raises him or her horizontally as high as the smallest member of the group can reach.

The group gently swings the volunteer back and forth like a falling leaf and slowly lowers the person to the floor. This stage should not be hurried. Have the person guess where the floor is and when he or she will get there.

Begin with the lightest member of the group and work up gradually to the heaviest member. Have the adults in your group do the exercise—if the group is physically able and the adults are willing.

Fourth Challenge: Trust Falls

Start with a single, sturdy chair. Have someone assigned to brace it for safety. The volunteer stands on the chair, facing away from the group, and assumes the stance: eyes closed, arms crossed, rigid body. The group forms two facing lines behind the volunteer.

For the single-chair drop, the group may kneel; the volunteer's feet should be slightly lower than the groups' arms. The group holds their arms in a "zipper" formation (alternating). They do not link arms.

The volunteer initiates the Ready signal and falls backwards. The group catches and then uprights the person. Start with the lighter members and work up to the heavier members.

Repeat the procedure using a sturdy table to gain more height for the fall, if you choose. But this time have the group stand to catch the volunteer.

Debrief

Have the group sit on the floor; then ask:

* What was that like for you?
* Which activity was the most fun? Why?
* Which was the scariest or the most difficult? What made it so?
* Which activities required trust?
* Why is trust important?
* What makes trust difficult?

Faith Link

Read the Scriptures; then ask :

* What do faith and trust have to do with each other?
* Why was trust important for Abraham?
* Why is trust important to us as Christians?
* What does it have to do with our group being together?

Wandering in the Wilderness

Supplies or Equipment:

Blindfolds, rope or bungee cords; large objects, such as chairs or other furniture

Focus: *Trust, perseverance in the face of frustration and obstacles*

Core Teaching: *God calls us to have faith—to trust. God's ways are not always the easiest, but they are the best. If we trust God's guidance and follow it, no matter how difficult it may be, it will ultimately lead us to where we want to go.*

Scripture: *Numbers 32:10-13 (The Israelites will wander in the wilderness.)*

The LORD's anger was kindled on that day and he swore, saying, "Surely none of the people who came up out of Egypt, from twenty years old and upward, shall see the land that I swore to give to Abraham, to Isaac, and to Jacob, because they have not unreservedly followed me—none except Caleb son of Jephunneh the Kenizzite and Joshua son of Nun, for they have unreservedly followed the LORD." And the LORD's anger was kindled against Israel, and he made them wander in the wilderness for forty years, until all the generation that had done evil in the sight of the LORD had disappeared.

Matthew 7:13-14 (The gate is narrow that leads to life.)

"Enter through the narrow gate; for the gate is wide and the road is easy that leads to destruction, and there are many who take it. For the gate is narrow and the road is hard that leads to life, and there are few who find it."

Group size: unlimited; extra adults to monitor the maze

Space: Indoors or outdoors; large area

Preparation

❏ Set up a maze using rope or bungees and objects. If you do the exercise outside, use trees. If you do it inside, you may want to use furniture.
❏ Use the drawing below to help you lay out a course. Put three entrances side by side. One

---

will lead in a long—but relatively straight—path to the exit. Place some obstacles near the entrance to make it appear more difficult. The other two paths will appear shorter, but both lead to dead ends.

❏ Position extra adults around the maze, have them watch for people who may wander out of the maze or who get frustrated.

❏ Secretly solicit the aid of two other persons to make comments (see the NOTE).

The Challenge

Blindfold your group members, then walk them to the area where you have created the maze, and give them the following instructions:

Welcome to the Wilderness Maze. Your goal is to find the exit. There are several entrances and several paths. But there is only one exit. Like Abraham and Israel of old, you are called on a journey of faith. You have four instructions:

1. You are to maintain contact with a rope at all times.
2. You are not to go under any ropes.
3. Go slowly. Keep one hand in front of you so you do not hit any obstacles.
4. You may go forward or backward.

As you begin, you will find several entrances. I recommend that you take the one on the left.

NOTE:
Have at least two other people say out loud that they do not think that the route to the left is a good idea, that all this path will do is "walk you into a dead end or a pile of trash."

The Process

Lead individuals to the entrances. Ask them each to make a choice. Then start them on their way.

As the participants find the exit, tap them on the shoulder. Have them remove the blindfold and quietly watch the rest of the group try to make it out of the maze.

The Key

Persons on the correct path will encounter obstacles that seem to make the path more difficult. However, in reality it is the only path that gets to the goal (the exit). The obstacles on the correct path should be substantial. The person on this path should have some degree of difficulty in getting through the obstacles. The other two paths seem easier, but they are dead ends.

Debrief

After the group has finished, have them sit in a circle by the maze; ask:

• What was this experience like for you?
• What did you feel like when you were in the maze?
• What did you find frustrating?

- What kept some of us from making it to the exit?
- How were those of you who made it able to find the exit?
- How did you handle the instruction to go to the left?
- How did you handle the other voices saying that they did not think the left was a good idea?
- How did you deal with any obstacles you ran into?
- What was the secret to success in this exercise?

Faith Link

Have a volunteer read aloud the passage from Numbers. Briefly relate the context of the story to your group:

Moses is reminding the people of their history and of the earlier generation's lack of faith. The distance from Egypt to the Promised Land was relatively short. The Israelites could have made the trip in a few weeks. However, they listened to the ten spies who reported that the natives of the Promised Land were gigantic and ferocious—rather than to the two, Joshua and Caleb, who urged them to trust God's promise and go ahead (Numbers 13–14).

The people whined and complained; they wanted to go back to Egypt. Because of their lack of faith, the Israelites had to wander in the wilderness for forty years before God allowed them to enter the Promised Land. (Forty years later, in order to enter the Promised Land, the new generation had to face the same giants and defeat them.)

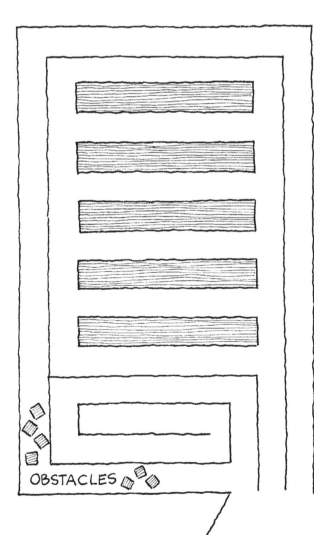

After you have explained the context of the Scripture, ask:

- How true-to-life do you find this portrait of the Israelite people? How are we like or unlike them?
- Do we find it difficult to trust? Why or why not?
- Where in your life do you sense obstacles or fears are blocking you?
- What obstacles do you experience?
- What voices do you encounter that encourage you not to take the path that has been suggested?
- What did you learn from this exercise that you could apply to your own life?

Read aloud Matthew 7:13-14; ask:

- What do you think this passage means?
- Why do you think the road that leads to destruction is easy and the gate wide?
- Why do you think the road that leads to life is hard and the gate narrow?
- How do you find this to be true in real life?

The Welcome

Focus: *Making others feel welcome*

Core Teaching: *God invites all into the community of faith. However, when new people come into our fellowship, the group is no longer the same. That can be difficult. As Christians, we are called to adapt and change so that those who are new might find a welcome place among us.*

Supplies or Equipment:
Platform, 3 feet square, 6 inches high; rope (Option 1) or platform, 2 feet square, 6 inches high (Option 2)

Scripture: *Romans 15:1-7 (Welcome one another as Christ has welcomed you.)*

We who are strong ought to put up with the failings of the weak, and not to please ourselves. Each of us must please our neighbor for the good purpose of building up the neighbor. For Christ did not please himself; but, as it is written, "The insults of those who insult you have fallen on me." For whatever was written in former days was written for our instruction, so that by steadfastness and by the encouragement of the scriptures we might have hope. May the God of steadfastness and encouragement grant you to live in harmony with one another, in accordance with Christ Jesus, so that together you may with one voice glorify the God and Father of our Lord Jesus Christ.

Welcome one another, therefore, just as Christ has welcomed you, for the glory of God.

Group size: 8–10 persons; additional adults to monitor safety

Space: Outdoors or indoors; area for an overhead rope swing (Option 1)

Preparation

There are two ways to do this activity, but the teaching content is the same. Your preparation will depend on which option you choose.

If you choose Option 1, securely fasten a rope to a tree or overhead object so that the group can swing to the platform. Option 2 does not require any additional apparatus. For Option 1 have an adult where the group is swinging from and an adult to monitor for safety at the platform where the group is swinging to. Option 2 requires only one adult per group. Other adults should participate.

The Challenge

The challenge is to get everyone on the platform at the same time. The participants must be touching one another, and they must remain on the platform for a slow count to ten (about three seconds) without falling.

The Process

If possible, use Option 1. Your group will enjoy the swinging activity, and the swinging brings a greater degree of difficulty in welcoming new members.

Option 1

Have two or three members of the group swing over to the platform. Keep bringing people across until it becomes next to impossible to hold everyone. The basic idea is that those who are on the platform will find it increasingly difficult to accommodate the late arrivals. Have your adults make mental notes of the comments group members make as the exercise becomes increasingly difficult.

Option 2

Have a volunteer step up on the platform. Congratulate the person for a job well done. Then have the volunteer choose a friend to be with him or her on the platform. Congratulate both of them. Have the newest person add someone else. Continue adding one individual at a time until everyone in the small group is on the platform. With each addition, the activity will become more difficult.

Debrief

Have the group sit in a circle around the platform; ask:

* What was that like for you?
* What was difficult about this experience?
* How did adding new members affect your goal of standing on the platform?
* What did you try that did not work?
* What did you try that did work?
* What were the keys to success?

Faith Link

Have someone read aloud Romans 15:1-7, then ask:

* What does the exercise we just did have to do with what Paul is talking about?
* What do you like about our youth group (or church, or class, or group)?
* What happens when new members come? How does it affect our group? How does it make closeness more difficult?
* What changes or accommodations do we need to make to welcome new people?
* How good are we at doing that?
* What could we do to do a better job of welcoming new people?

Where to Go for More

Resources

For more than 25 years Project Adventure, Inc., has been the leading organization in the Adventure Education field. They publish books, provide training workshops, design challenge courses, and sell equipment. They have catalogs (800-796-9917).

QuickSilver: Adventure Games, Initiative Problems, Trust Activities and a Guide to Effective Leadership, by Karl Rohnke and Steve Butler (Project Adventure, Inc., 1995). 150 new games and activities, plus a helpful section on leadership.

Cowstails and Cobras II: A Guide to Games, Initiatives, Ropes Courses, & Adventure Curriculum. A classic by Karl Rohnke (Project Adventure, Inc., 1989).

Silver Bullets: A Guide to Initiative Problems, Adventure Games and Trust Activities, by Karl Rohnke (Project Adventure, Inc., 1984) 165 activites, each requiring few, if any, props.

Youth Leadership in Action: A Guide to Cooperative Games and Group Activities, Written by and for Youth Leaders (Project Adventure, Inc.).

Building Community in Youth Groups, by Denny Rydberg (Group, 1985)

Trust Builders, by Denny Rydberg (Group, 1993)

Up Close and Personal, by Mike Yaconelli (Youth Specialties)

Also by Walt Marcum

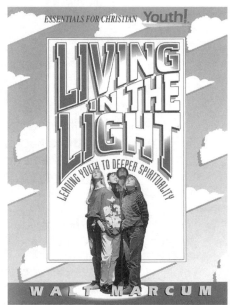

Living in the Light: Leading Youth to Deeper Spirituality (Abingdon Press, 1994). Proven ideas and techniques from a veteran youth minister: 19 Bible study techniques that work with youth, 34 prayer techniques for speaking to and listening to God, a focus on worship, and a spiritual life retreat. (0-687-39235-7)

Credits

Abraham's Journey: The original idea for this activity came from Sherpa Walk (page 89 of *Silver Bullets*) The idea of a trust walk is generic. The idea I used from Sherpa Walk was having the guide not use words. The rest of the activity I created.

Abyss: This activity is in the Youth Specialities book *Up Close and Personal*. I have kept the exercise basically intact. The idea of adding the third piece of tape and calling it a razor-sharp piece of rock is mine, as is the Faith Link.

Bear One Another's Burdens: This lesson uses three activities that have been around for a while.

Corporate Connection: This is a Project Adventure game (page 149 of *Quicksilver*). We use the kits that can be purchased from Project Adventure. All of the debriefing and Faith Link is mine.

Count the Cost: This is a variation on a Project Adventure activity, Key Punch (pages 167-169 of *Quicksilver*).

Diminishing Resources: I have never seen this activity in a book. I learned this activity from Billy and Laura Echols-Richter at a retreat in Oklahoma about 12 years ago. Billy and Laura are on staff at St. Andrews United Methodist Church in Plano, Texas. They are also certified in ropes challenge initiatives.

End of Your Rope: These activities have a variety of sources, including Project Adventure (a variation on Yurt Circle, page 258 of *Quicksilver*); I learned the End of Your Rope activity at Adventure Experiences in Taylor Park, CO.

Escape From Auschwitz: This is my variation on the old Electric Fence idea.

Eye of the Needle: This is a variation of the old Porthole activity that has been around for years. Porthole is a lower ropes course standard.

Four Balls: I learned this activity from Billy and Laura Echols-Richter about 12 years ago.

Islands: This is another lower ropes course standard. Sometimes it is called Islands. I have also hear it called Mountaintop (with a different fantasy—a plane crashed on a mountain top).

Lifeline and Unseen Hands: Again, I learned these activities from Billy and Laura Echols-Richter.

Moses at the Red Sea: This is my adaptation of another lower ropes standard. Sometimes it is called Chocolate River, The Swamp, or Stepping Stones.

Owl Island: The basic idea is in the Youth Specialities book, Up Close and Personal. The debrief and Faith Link are mine.

River Crossing: This one is found of pages 75-76 of *Adventure Recreation 2.*

Shepherd's Voice: I used ideas that have been around in a variety of ways. This formulation is mine.

Space Web: I have never seen this activity in a book. I learned the activity while at Adventure Experiences in Taylor Park, Colorado. They said at the time that it was not original to them. They had learned it from someone else. I have made substantial changes to the activity and the setting it is placed in is mine. Adventure Experiences is the main builder of ropes challenge courses in America.

Spider Web: This is another lower ropes course standard. I have used the activity in the traditional way, though the setting and debrief are my own.

Squares: The basic activity is from *Community Building in Youth Ministry,* by Denny Ryberg (Group). The rest of the curriculum setting is mine.

3D Minefield: This one is a Project Adventure activity (pages 146–147 of Quicksilver). I have changed the activity somewhat, allowing the guide to be in the minefield with the blindfolded person.

Toxic Waste: This is a Project Adventure activity (page 187 of *Quicksilver*). I added all the curriculum aspects.

Trust Exercises: Again, these are standard. They are found in Project Adventure books and are done at most ropes courses, as well as other places. I learned these activities at a United Methodist camp years ago. The exact way we do them is unique to us.

Wandering in the Wilderness: This is my activity. It just takes the general maze idea and uses it. The five rules I took from The Maze found on page 103–104 of *Cowstails and Cobras II*, a Project Adventure book.

The Welcome: The two options use two lower ropes challenge activities that have been around forever. Option One is a variation on Nitro Crossing, a ropes standard. Option Two is another lower ropes standard, called All Aboard. The idea of beginning with one person and then having that person choose the next person, as well as the rest of the curriculum surrounding the activity, is mine.

Your Handy-Dandy Indexes

The Bible in Go For It!

Genesis 1:26-31a (God charges humankind to care for creation.) Toxic Waste

Genesis 12:1-5 (Abraham trusts God.) Trust Exercises

Genesis 12:1-9 (Abram trusts God's leading.) Abraham's Journey

Exodus 14:10-22 (Moses gets God's help in crossing the Red Sea.) Moses and the Red Sea

Numbers 11:11-17 (God gives Moses help with the people.) Diminishing Resources

Numbers 32:10-13 (The Israelites will wander in the wilderness.) Wandering in the Wilderness

1 Samuel 3:1-10 (Samuel hears God's call.) Abraham's Journey

1 Kings 19:1-8 (The prophet Elijah comes to the end of his rope.) The End of Your Rope

1 Kings 19:13-18 (Elijah feels alone.)Diminishing Resources

Psalm 23 (The Lord is my shepherd.) The Shepherd's Voice

Ecclesiastes 3:1-8 (There is a time for everything.) Spider Web

Ecclesiastes 4:9-12 (Two are better than one.) River Crossing, 3D Minefield

Isaiah 48:10 (I have tested you.) The Abyss

Matthew 7:13-14 (The gate is narrow.) Wandering in the Wilderness

Matthew 19:16-26 (It is hard for persons encumbered with possessions to enter the kingdom of heaven.) Eye of the Needle

Mark 9:33-37 (Whoever would be greatest must be servant of all.) Squares

Luke 10:25-28 (We are called by God to love one another.) Name Game and Do You Like Your Friends?

Luke 10:25-28 (Love God with your whole being.) Space Web

Luke 14:27-32 (Whoever does not carry the cross … cannot be my disciple) Count the Cost

John 8:12 (Follow me, and you will not walk in darkness.) Lifeline and Unseen Hands

John 10:6-18 (The Good Shepherd) The Shepherd's Voice

John 13:3-15 (Jesus washes the feet of the disciples.) Squares

Romans 4:4-5 (Abraham's trust is an example for us.) Trust Exercises

Romans 5:3-5 (Suffering produces endurance … hope.)The Abyss

Romans 12:3-8 (We have gifts that differ, but we are members one of another.) Islands

Romans 15:1-7 (Welcome one another as Christ has welcomed you.) The Welcome

1 Corinthians 12:4-9 (God gives each of us different gifts—for the common good.) Owl Island

1 Corinthians 12:13-21 (In the body all parts are equally important and needed.) The Corporate Connection, Four Balls

2 Corinthians 4:8-16a (We do not lose heart.) The Abyss

Galatians 6:2 (Bear one another's burdens.) Bear One Another's Burdens

Ephesians 4:1-7 (Each of us was given grace.) Bear One Another's Burdens

Hebrews 12:1 (Run the race with perseverance.) Eye of the Needle

1 John 1:4-7 (God is light; walk in the light.) Lifeline and Unseen Hands

1 John 3:13-18 (Let us love in truth and action.) Escape From Auschwitz

1 John 4:20-21 (We cannot love God without loving people.) Name Game and Do You Like Your Friends? Space Web